The Climate Diet

The Climate Diet

How You Can Cut Carbon, Cut Costs, and Save the Planet

Jonathan Harrington

publishing for a sustainable future

London • Sterling, VA

First Published by Earthscan in the UK and USA in 2008

ISBN: 978-1-84407-533-1

Typeset by Safehouse Creative
Printed and bound by The Maple-Vail Book Manufacturing Group, York, Pennsylvania, USA
Illustrations by Dan Bramall
Cover design by Rob Watts

For a full list of publications please contact:

Earthscan
Dunstan House, 14A St Cross Street,
London EC1N 8XA
Tel: +44 (0)20 7841 1930
Fax: +44 (0)20 7242 1474
Email: earthinfo@earthscan.co.uk
Web: www.earthscan.co.uk

22883 Quicksilver Drive, Sterling, VA 20166-2012, USA

Earthscan publishes in association with the International Institute for Environment and Development

A catalog record for this book is available from the British Library.

Library of Congress Cataloging-in-Publication Data

Harrington, Jonathan Henry, 1964–
    The climate diet : how you can cut carbon, cut costs and save the planet / Jonathan Harrington.
        p. cm.
    Includes bibliographical references and index.
    ISBN-13: 978-1-84407-533-1 (pbk.)
    1. Climatic changes. 2. Global warming–Prevention. 3. Carbon dioxide–Environmental aspects. 4. Greenhouse gases–Environmental aspects. I. Title.
    QC981.8.C5H2567 2008
    640–dc22
                                                                            2008003018

This book has been printed on paper that is 30% recycled from post-consumer waste using vegetable-based inks.

For Kela

So she too may have an opportunity to enjoy
the rich bounty of our Mother Earth

Contents

Appendices

List of Acronyms and Abbreviations

ATV   all terrain vehicle
bpd   barrels per day
Btu   British thermal unit
C   Celsius
CFL   compact fluorescent lamp
CH_4 methane
cm   centimeter
CO_2 carbon dioxide
CO_2e carbon dioxide equivalent
cu ft   cubic feet
E-85   85% ethanol/15% gasoline fuel
EC   European Commission
EER   energy-efficient ratio
EIA   Energy Information Administration
EPA   Environmental Protection Agency (USA)
EU   European Union
F   Fahrenheit
g   gram
gal   gallon
GHG   greenhouse gas
gpm   gallons per minute
hp   horsepower
IEA   International Energy Agency
IPCC   Intergovernmental Panel on Climate Change
IISD   International Institute for Sustainable Development
kg   kilogram
km   kilometer
km/h   kilometers per hour
kWh   kilowatt hour
lb   pound/pounds (U.S.)
LCD   liquid crystal display
LED   light-emitting diode
LEED   Leadership in Energy and Environmental Design
L/m   liter per minute
m   meter

mi	mile
mpg	miles per gallon
mph	miles per hour
N_2O	nitrous oxide
NOAA	National Oceanic and Atmospheric Administration
PC	per capita
ppm	parts per million
SEER	seasonal energy-efficient ratio
sq ft	square feet
sq m	square meters
TCO	total cost of ownership
UK	United Kingdom
U.S.	United States
W	watt

List of Tables

Acknowledgments

First of all, I would like to thank my aunt and uncle, Belden and Lisa Paulson, for allowing me to vicariously participate in their decades-long crusade to save the planet. Their hard work and vision has affected the lives of thousands of people. I would like to thank my parents, Mary Paulson and Gordon Harrington, for giving me the gift of education that has allowed me to contribute to public debates about environmental politics and policy. Special thanks to my wife, Kathy, who taught me to walk more softly on the planet, through actions not words, and to rein in the disease of "affluenza" that infects modern society. I certainly could not have reached this point without my editor, Rob West, who believed in this project from beginning to end and pushed me to persevere though months of rewrites. Many people and organizations provided helpful comments and material assistance during the course of this project, including the Wunderkids at Verve Editorial, Northwest Avalanche Center, Ted and Bunny Belden, Stylus Publishing marketing staff, Mary Ann Acosta, the University of Washington Puget Sound Action Team staff, Dr. Ken Stiles, Dr. Paul Harris, David Lagerman, Waverly Fitzgerald, and all of my global-warming-doubting graduate students who challenged me to defend my values over the years. I would also like to express many thanks to all the sales associates who have put up with my pesky questions about product energy efficiency (questions that surprisingly few people ask). Finally, I would like especially to thank my daughter, Kela, who inspired me to write this book. Nothing makes clearer the meaning of the word *responsibility* than parenthood. To a large extent, her future is in our hands. And I am determined not to mess it up.

Jonathan Henry Harrington
January 2008

Preface

This project started out as an academic tome. I was one year away from applying for tenure at my university and knew that the academic powers that be would prefer a book written for an academic audience. Academia is a Byzantine, mysterious world full of unwritten rules and codes. Academic writing is also, by nature, full of jargon and largely inaccessible to the average person. Well, like most people, I did not finish the book when I expected to. Life, as they say, got in the way. Fortunately, I got tenure anyway. So now I can write the book I wanted to write, a book that expresses my love for nature and serious concerns about how the specter of global warming endangers our future. I also provide real strategies all of us can use in our daily lives to combat climate change.

A common phrase people in the environmental movement use to express the core motivation behind mass activism is NIMBY (not in my backyard). Not surprisingly, most people are motivated to act against threats they perceive to affect themselves, their family, neighbors, and/or community directly. Unfortunately, global warming is not yet viewed by many as a current, personal threat. Most see the climate crisis as someone else's problem; something that governments, states, and international organizations should fix.

One of the main goals of this book is to dispel this misconception. Global warming *is* in our backyard. The reality is that the aggregate actions of millions of individuals is a primary engine behind our present climate crisis. We all share some personal responsibility to modify the way we live—to reduce our use of fossil fuel–based energy, products, and services that produce the greenhouse gases that are warming our world. The lifestyle that we so lovingly embrace is literally robbing our own children of their fundamental right to share in the Earth's bounty. However, if enough of us act in unison to combat this problem, we collectively have the power to avoid the most serious local and global consequences of uncontrolled climate change.

Cool Strategies for a Warming World

1

Climate change. The subject seems to be coming up a lot these days. Everyone is talking about it; major news organizations, Hollywood elites, congressmen and members of Parliament, presidents, and prime ministers have finally joined the chorus of experts and activists who have long worried about this global threat. Concerned citizens, from the concrete canyons of Shanghai to the arid flatlands of Alice Springs, Australia, are also fast coming to the realization that something is just not right with our planet's climate (Rosenthal and Revkin, 2007).

Weird weather patterns are popping up everywhere. Each year seems hotter than the last. The frequency and intensity of hurricanes is increasing. The winter/spring of 2006–2007 was no exception. In January 2007 thousands shed their winter gear and flocked to New York City's Central Park, where temperatures soared above 70° F (21° C; *New York Times*, 2007). A few days later, the city was blanketed with snow. Seattle, a town known for getting lots of precipitation, experienced the rainiest November in its history. Australian farmers in the Murray-Darling River Basin, home to 40% of the country's total agricultural output, faced catastrophic losses because of severe water shortages brought about by years of drought (*The Economist*, 2007). Severe drought conditions also engulfed many parts of the southeastern United States, forcing many farmers to abandon their crops, and stimulated conflicts among governors and other regional leaders over water rights. Thousands of Arctic residents now watch helplessly as their homes sink into the ground because the permafrost on which they are built is slowly melting away (*Science Daily*, 2007).

Yet even with so much mounting evidence, many still ask:

- ✓ What is global warming?
- ✓ What causes it and why is it so bad?
- ✓ And if it is really such a threat, is there anything we can do to stop it?

The Climate Diet: How You Can Cut Carbon, Cut Costs, and Save the Planet provides clear and easy answers to each of these questions. Yes, global warming is a real threat, both now and in the future. Yes, our energy-intensive lifestyles are partly to blame for the greenhouse gases (GHGs; the main ones are carbon dioxide [CO_2], methane [CH_4], and

Global warming is a real threat, both now and in the future.

nitrous oxide [N_2O]) that form the ever-thickening "blanket" that is warming our world. But the good news is that we still have time to act. If we can just cut back on our use of carbon-based fossil fuels, such as coal, oil, natural gas, and others, we can slow the march of human-caused climate change—one individual, family, and community at a time.

What we really need to do is go on a diet: a Climate Diet. *The Climate Diet* provides all the information individuals need to know about global warming and shows you how a few simple lifestyle changes can reduce your household carbon footprint by more than 32,000 pounds (14,528 kg) or 40% and slash your yearly energy bill by more than $1,600 or 46%. Ready to save the atmosphere and lots of money? Read on to learn more about how you can start *your* own Climate Diet.

Climate Change: What You Need to Know

Most of us live in a world of excess. We consume too much of everything: clothes, shoes, toys, electronic gadgets, home decor, yard accoutrements, and bricks and mortar. At times it seems as though manic shopping has replaced football as our national sport. We are also obsessed with the wonderful world of food, and yet there, too, we suffer the consequences of overindulgence. Lifestyle-influenced diseases such as Type II Diabetes, obesity, and lung cancer kill hundreds of thousands of people each year and sicken millions more. Our bodies just cannot take it anymore.

Our overuse of her resources is not only killing us, but is also destroying the larger body that sustains us.

And we are not the only ones getting sick. Over time, Mother Earth has done a fairly good job of keeping herself healthy without human intervention. She provides for the myriad life forms that inhabit every nook and cranny of her being. But six billion people, like a force of nature, are altering the landscape. Our overuse of her resources, or "bingeing" if you will, is not only killing us, but is also destroying the larger "body" that sustains us. Through Mother Earth's veins (rivers and streams) flows water clogged with toxic waste. Her beautiful face (surface) is pockmarked with freeways, high-rises and apartment buildings, strip malls, and landfills. And her lungs (our atmosphere) are awash in pollution. Ozone-depleting substances have stripped away her defenses against ultraviolet radiation.

But the greatest threat of all to her health is our overuse of carbon-based energy sources like oil and coal. By overusing these resources, we are upsetting the delicate system that controls temperature on the planet. This system, the *carbon cycle*, which regulates carbon levels in the atmosphere, on land, in oceans, and in sedimentary deposits, is being thrown out of whack. For eons, Mother Earth has safely stored most of her rich bounty of carbon, including fossil fuels in liquid, gaseous, and solid forms, on top of or underneath the Earth's surface or in bodies of water. Only a tiny sliver, less than 1%, of our atmosphere is made up of carbon dioxide, methane, and other heat-trapping gases, which are instrumental in keeping terrestrial temperatures fairly stable.

> The **carbon cycle**, which regulates carbon levels in the atmosphere, on land, in oceans, and in sedimentary deposits, is being thrown out of whack.

This so-called greenhouse effect has long protected us from the bitter cold of outer space while keeping our planet warm enough to be hospitable to life and the development of human civilization . . . until now (Appenzeller and Dimick, 2004). Our burning of fossil fuels (about 84 million barrels of oil a day [bpd] in 2006!) is spewing too much carbon dioxide into the atmosphere. Without urgent action, the International Energy Agency (IEA) predicts that worldwide oil consumption could increase to over 116 million bpd, while overall primary energy needs increase 55% over 2005 levels by 2030 (IEA, 2007). The result is that the Earth's paper-thin layer of heat-trapping gases is simply becoming too dense. Temperatures are now within 3.6° F (2° C) of being the warmest they have been in a million years. So, just like someone turning up the heat on an electric blanket, higher GHG concentrations further warm our world (for more information about the science behind human-induced climate change, check out Appendix A).

> Temperatures are now within 3.6° F (2° C) of being the warmest they have been in a million years.

Kids in an Ice Cream Shop

It is clear that a climate crisis is already upon us. So why have we not done more to address this global threat? When it comes to using carbon-based fossil fuels, most of us are like kids in an ice cream shop: It's there, we want it, and we want it *now*. If we have the money to pay for it, what's the problem? President George W. Bush hit the nail on the head when he noted in his 2006 State of the Union address that "America is addicted to oil" (Bush, 2006). Though generally less severe, this same addiction applies to most industrialized countries. We lunge left and right for the tastiest treats like there is no tomorrow. Imagine our society placing its order: "Sir, I would like a chocolate-covered, mocha sundae. No, make that two. And throw in two banana splits and a double-fudge brownie. And don't forget the whipped cream! Also, could you add some of those little rainbow sprinkles? And, of course, no sundae is complete without a cherry on top!"

OK. So we all go overboard once in awhile. Some of us surely remember long nights that might follow days of overindulgence. Yes, it is true that our bodies can take a certain amount of punishment in the short term. However, the real problem starts when overeating becomes a daily event.

1   Suddenly, you find that your old clothes don't fit.

2   You feel tired and sick.

3   Your cholesterol and blood pressure shoot up.

4   You load up on drugs to fix these maladies, but then the drugs themselves start causing new health problems.

5   Chronic diseases set in.

6   Plaque clogs your arteries. Then . . .

Just like that "spare tire" around your waist that never seems to go away, global warming is here to stay unless we change our lifestyles.

Global warming follows a similar course. Like a slowly developing illness, it sneaks up on us almost unnoticed. What's the harm in buying that third SUV, building a monstrous house, or flying to Paris for the weekend? Why should you walk to the store to buy a loaf of bread when you can drive? We turn up the heat or blast the air conditioner in our homes and cars with abandon. Each and every one of these actions contributes to global warming. And what do you think happens when you take your own GHG emissions and multiply them by a billion? After decades of overconsumption, real long-term problems crop up. So, just like that "spare tire" around your waist that never seems to go away, global warming is here to stay unless we change our lifestyles.

The Climate Diet

At some point, something just has to give. We either need to take steps to put our personal and planetary systems back into balance or be prepared to suffer the consequences. So, what do God-fearing, unhealthy, overweight thirty- or forty-somethings do when the doctor tells them they are eating themselves into an early grave? Go on a diet! That is what I am asking you to do.

Now—lights, camera, action! I am pleased to have this opportunity to introduce to you my Gold Medal Plan to dieting success! This plan includes six steps: (1) Get the facts, (2) Make a decision, (3) Set goals, (4) Count your (carbon) calories, (5) Get involved, and (6) Evaluate and monitor. My Gold Medal Plan also offers four different participation levels: Participant, Bronze, Silver, and Gold, each of which can be tailored to fit almost any lifestyle.

Let's look at my **six-step** plan to dieting success:

1. Get the facts.
It is important for all of us to educate ourselves about why we should be more sensitive to how our lifestyles affect others. Drawing from my own family's experiences and the latest scientific research, I present a compelling case for why we should care about human-caused climate change. The main reason is that *global warming is happening here and now*. It is right in our backyard. Its effects are everywhere: near my home in the Seattle area, among the concrete spires of Shanghai, and in the nether reaches of Greenland. It is a truly global phenomenon that demands immediate attention from all of us.

Global warming is right in our backyard.

2. Make a decision.
The saddest thing about global warming is that our actions not only have an impact on our own lives, but have an even bigger effect on people in other parts of the world and on future generations. Consider taking personal responsibility for your impact on the climate. Teach your children to live a more sustainable lifestyle. Be better stewards of the planet. There is nothing we can do about the past. The important thing is that we try to remedy the situation and avoid repeating our mistakes.

Consider taking personal responsibility for your impact on the climate.

3. Set goals.

Each household should work as a unit to establish goals everyone can live with but will also lead to meaningful cuts in the family's impact on the climate. We can all do something.

4. Count your (carbon) calories.

Now comes the exciting part, taking action. "Going for the Gold: The Nuts and Volts of Carbon Dieting Success" (chapter 3) will introduce you to easy-to-use methods to determine your family's impact on the environment. The following chapters provide specific suggestions about what you can do to cut your carbon footprint at home (chapters 4 and 5), when shopping (chapter 6), on the road (chapter 7), and in the community (chapter 8). The book provides three dieting plans: the Shortest-Cut Diet Plan, the Shortcut Diet Plan, and the Full House Audit and Comprehensive Diet Plan. The Climate Diet also includes hundreds of helpful tips on how to get your home interior, yard, food and waste, shopping, and transportation choices in order. You will be amazed at how small lifestyle changes can bring benefits to the atmosphere and your pocketbook.

5. Get involved.

Dieting usually works best when you do it with a friend. Consider starting a neighborhood or church discussion group, join an environmental organization, vote for climate-friendly candidates, or participate in community activities geared toward helping to minimize climate impacts. Lobby government entities to plan more efficient communities and provide public transportation, and reignite your commitment to the common good, locally and globally (see chapter 8).

6. Evaluate and monitor.

Did you achieve your planned dieting milestones? Chapter 9, "Putting It All Together: *Your* Climate Diet Results" provides a framework for determining how you did. It allows you to evaluate your strengths and weaknesses, and it summarizes suggestions made throughout the book that you can use to maintain and improve your Climate Diet outcomes.

Learn easy-to-use methods to determine your family's impact on the environment.

You will be amazed at how small lifestyle changes can bring benefits to the atmosphere and your pocketbook.

How Much Should We Cut?

Scientists have developed some pretty good predictions about how much we need to cut GHG emissions to get our climate back into shape. Let's make this really simple:

In my book you get credit for doing something, however small, but progressively better rewards are provided for those who do more. Like many kids, my daughter loves the visual arts. She also regularly participates in art competitions. She gets a kick out of covering her bookshelf with ribbons, statuettes, and medals. Fortunately for her, in this day and age it is almost impossible not to get some kind of award just for getting involved. Like many kids, most of her ribbons are "participation" awards. However, the prizes she *really* covets are medals: bronze, silver, and gold. Medaling, for her, is what really separates the women from the girls. For many of us, medals won are a testament to our commitment, hard work, and dedication to our craft or cause— whatever it may be. In any case, whether you choose to be a Participant or go for the Gold, be sure that every little bit counts!

Participant Award

This award goes to anyone who does something, *anything*, to reduce his or her GHG emissions, for example, turning off the lights when leaving a room, walking rather than driving to the store, or installing compact fluorescent lightbulbs in the bathroom. Every little bit does count, and this award encourages any effort.

Bronze Medal

This is the next step: your first chance at a medal. The Intergovernmental Panel on Climate Change (IPCC), the premier body responsible for dissecting the science behind climate change, recommends that developed countries cut their GHG emissions between 5% and 10% below 1990 levels as a first step to stabilizing global carbon dioxide levels. For most people in developed countries, achieving this goal requires about a 25% or 30% reduction from where we are now. So in the near term, every family should shoot for this goal. Unlike your college calculus grade, lower is always better (IPCC, 2001, 2007). Cut 25% and you get a Bronze Medal. You will be amazed at how easy it is to achieve.

Silver Medal

If you can cut your GHG emissions by half you will be well on your way to demonstrating your personal commitment to save the atmosphere and the world's scarce resources for future generations, and you'll earn yourself a Silver Medal to boot. Few families will be able to do this overnight. As with any diet, substantial lifestyle changes require a bit of planning and dedication. But a 50% reduction is certainly doable. Germany's per capita carbon dioxide emissions are about half those in the United States and Canada. If they can do it, anyone can (Baumert, Herzog, and Pershing, 2005).

Gold Medal

We humans collectively need to cut emissions by more than 60% below 1990 levels.

Gold! No medal is more coveted. Earning a Gold Medal shows the world that you have reached the pinnacle of success. Scientists say that to ensure long-term global temperature stability, we humans collectively need to cut emissions by more than 60% below 1990 levels. For Americans or Canadians, this translates to more than a 75% reduction. Sound impossible? Well, get this: In 2005 three-quarters of the world's population produced more than 75% fewer GHGs per person than the average American consumer (World Resources Institute [WRI], 2006). We *can* do this if we put our minds to it.

Ultimately, the ideal we should all be shooting for is real *sustainable development*, that is, using energy and resources in ways that preserve them for future generations and do not injure others— either today or in the future. As alternative energy and conservation technologies progress, this goal is easier to achieve than ever. As with weight loss, the real challenge is mustering enough personal commitment to translate good wishes into concrete actions. It may look like a long road now, but I promise you, after you get there, you will never look back.

In summary, *The Climate Diet* is about making small incremental changes in the way you, your family, or your community inhabits this planet—changes that, over time, can accrue real environmental benefits. Numerous studies show that most successful dieters take a slow, gradual approach to changing their unhealthy behavior. Going cold turkey or practicing extreme self-denial of the things you love is rarely a successful way to lose weight or to cut GHG emissions. Each family has its own unique circumstances. We all have different values and interests. Any carbon-cutting strategy that does not take this into account is doomed to fail.

> Most successful dieters take a gradual approach to changing their unhealthy behavior.

Also, family members should avoid adopting a messianic attitude toward climate dieting by doling out the wrath of God on loved ones who do not share their zealous desire to save the biosphere. Households should adopt new lifestyle changes that everyone can agree with and work on as a unit. Cut what you can, when you can. If you really can't give up that gas-guzzling SUV at the moment, try cutting somewhere else. Make fewer trips to the store, vacation closer to home, or install a superefficient heating system. There are so many ways you can slash your climate-harming emissions. Pick the ones that are the most comfortable but still bring measurable environmental benefits.

> Adopt new lifestyle changes that everyone can agree with and work on together.

So what are you waiting for? It is time to start *your* Climate Diet!

Ten Good Reasons to Go On a Climate Diet

2

Do you still need a reason to start doing something about the climate crisis? We live in a world of lists: David Letterman's Top Ten, Steven Covey's Seven Habits, Yahweh's Ten Commandments. We love them. So, here is my own list of **ten good reasons** why you may want to consider going on a Climate Diet. I hope at least one of these arguments will motivate you to start along the path toward carbon emissions independence. I have deliberately avoided putting these in any particular order. It is up to you to decide which, if any, of these reasons is most important and appealing to you.

✔ Reason 1: Somebody has to do it!

✔ Reason 2: Our model of sustainable development is not sustainable.

✔ Reason 3: Global warming: It is in our backyard.

✔ Reason 4: Alleviate climate change–related suffering in the developing world.

✔ Reason 5: Rectify past mistakes.

✔ Reason 6: Be better stewards.

✔ Reason 7: Beat the "affluenza" bug.

✔ Reason 8: Save the commons.

✔ Reason 9: Save money.

✔ Reason 10: Save nature for its own sake.

Reason 1: Somebody Has to Do It!

Who is most at fault for all the environmental destruction wrought by human-caused climate change? Clearly the citizens of North America and Europe are overwhelmingly responsible for the historical GHG emissions that are now destroying our environment and endangering our children's future. And today, every time we jump into our cars, turn on a light, or take an airplane trip we continue to produce the GHGs that are warming our world (WRI, 2006).

It would be nice if we could just pass off the blame for climate change to elected officials or multinational corporations. Certainly they are

Greenhouse emissions regulations range from lax to almost nonexistent in most U.S. jurisdictions.

complicit in this enterprise; greenhouse emissions regulations range from lax to almost nonexistent in most U.S. jurisdictions (though a number of states have banded together to regulate carbon dioxide without federal oversight). This allows oil companies like BP, ExxonMobil, and Chevron, among others, to keep conducting business as usual in the United States even as they face increased scrutiny abroad. And while some European politicians make bold claims about how much progress they have made in adopting more climate-friendly policies, the gap between rhetoric and reality remains large.

At a European Union (EU) summit in March 2007, the leaders of France, Germany, the United Kingdom, and other member states extolled the "greenness" of their policies. However, details about how countries will implement these goals are few and far between (Parker, Bounds, and Benoit, 2007). Most of these nations have little hope of meeting already watered-down commitments of the Kyoto Protocol, which commits developed nation signatories to reduce GHG emissions below 1990 levels. Canada, which also signed the Kyoto Protocol, is not likely to live up to its emissions goals. Canadian emissions are increasing at an even faster rate than those of the United States (WRI, 2006). We should also remember that if EU leaders commit to and implement existing proposals, they are still far below what scientists say is necessary to significantly slow global warming.

Most nations have little hope of meeting the already watered-down Kyoto commitments

This issue goes way beyond everyday electoral politics. It is fundamentally a question of personal responsibility. We already noted the wide-ranging effects of human-induced climate change on Mother Earth and the billions of people who depend on her for their own survival. So at some point each of us needs to face up to the hard, simple fact that our energy-intensive and overconsumptive lifestyles are a direct cause of the current environmental crisis—and real change won't happen until we start making changes ourselves (as well as perhaps pressuring our lawmakers to do so). Somebody has to do it—why not you?

Reason 2: Our Model of Sustainable Development Is Not Sustainable

One excuse many of us may give for not adopting more climate-friendly lifestyles is that we think we are already doing enough to solve the problem. Political and social elites are partly to blame for fostering this misconception. Politicians love to talk about their support for "sustainable development." The most widely accepted definition of sustainable development is "development that meets the needs of the present generation without compromising the ability of future generations to meet their own needs" (Bruntland Commission, 1987). This concept includes three major elements:

✓ **First**, it links economy, environment, and equity into one comprehensive decision-making process.

✓ **Second**, it emphasizes long-term change and its impact on intergenerational equality.

✓ **Third**, it recognizes natural resource scarcity and the limited carrying capacities of ecosystems.

However, the truth is there is no such thing as sustainable development in the industrialized world. Every single country heavily depends on nonrenewable fossil fuels.

 The nation that comes closest to escaping this dependency is Iceland. Decades ago, the small island nation made a decision to develop a "geothermal" energy strategy. Because of its unusual geological features, Iceland is uniquely situated to take advantage of this energy resource. Much of the country's heating and electricity needs are well served by this renewable resource. Iceland is also pursuing wind and tidal power technologies.

 Even so, Iceland still must import about 70% of its energy needs to keep its economy growing (BBC, 2001). The case of Iceland aptly illustrates the wide gap that exists between the dream and the reality of sustainable development. This term is so misleading it is probably better to not even use it in reference to the world we live in today (Appenzeller, 2004).

> There is no such thing as sustainable development in the industrialized world.

Reason 3: Global Warming:
It Is in Our Backyard

Many of us worry about human-caused climate change in the abstract. However, we often do not view the climate crisis as a current personal threat. It is one thing to hear about floods, extreme weather, and desertification in other places, but it's quite another to have them happen in our own backyard. Well, the planet's atmosphere *is* in our own backyard. It knows no bounds, and changes are happening, right now, everywhere. One way we are experiencing this change is through global rising temperatures, with more dramatic increases in the upper latitudes.

Over the years my daughter, Kela, and my wife, Kathy, and I have had many backyards. Kathy is originally from Shanghai, China. I was born in Georgia, grew up in Utah, and went to college in Iowa. From there I moved to California, and then Taiwan where I lived for two years. Kathy and I met in Hawaii, where we both completed our master's degrees. She followed me to the Chicago area where I earned my doctorate. Kela, our pride and joy, was born in Evanston, Illinois. I had my first full-time teaching gig in Japan, where we lived for more than three years. I have visited all 50 U.S. states and over 35 countries. And while each of our backyards seems worlds apart, they all have one thing in common: climate change.

My family's current backyard is in Mercer Island, Washington. On a clear summer day, locals love to sit on their porches and behold the blue waters of Lake Washington, Mount Rainier, and the Cascades. The beauty of the Pacific Northwest can be truly breathtaking. On the surface, it seems that all is well. It is not.

In past years, extreme weather fluctuations have been playing havoc with the lives of Washingtonians. In early 2006 the state capital, Olympia, experienced 35 straight days of rain, a record even for the famously wet Pacific Northwest (National Oceanic and Atmospheric Administration [NOAA], 2006). But this is only the beginning of the story. That same year, the ski resort nearest to Seattle, the Summit at Snoqualmie in the Cascade Range, had its longest ski season in years. On March 15, 2006, 118 inches of snow were on the ground at the base of the main lodge. Not only were skiers ecstatic, but eastern Washington farmers were happy as well. They heavily depend on snowpack runoff to get them through the dry summer months (Northwest Weather and Avalanche Center [NWAC], 2006).

However, the 2005 ski season was a totally different story. On March 15, 2005, not a single inch of snow was on the ground at the base of the Summit at Snoqualmie. (NWAC, 2006). The problem was not just a lack of moisture. It was just too warm to snow. The ski season was a disaster. Hundreds of seasonal employees were laid off. Restaurants and hotels struggled to survive. And what about the farmers and their coveted snowpack-based water supply? They had to ration water and cut back production that spring and summer, causing millions of dollars in losses. Meanwhile, the state experienced one of its worst fire seasons on record. Nationally 8.5 million acres (3.44 million hectares) went up in smoke (National Climatic Data Center/National Oceanic and Atmospheric Administration [NCDC/NOAA], 2006).

Any weather forecaster will tell you that two years do not make a trend. However, scientists do have a good handle on Pacific Northwest weather patterns, with records going back hundreds of years. The wildly volatile weather of 2005 and 2006 is symptomatic of what Washingtonians can expect in the future as temperatures rise: alternating extreme weather events trending overall toward warmer winters with heavier rainfall and warming temperatures, followed by hotter, dryer summers (Saunders and Maxwell, 2005). If temperatures continue to rise as projected, skiing may disappear from the list of local pastimes along Washington's Cascade Range corridor in coming decades.

Reason 4: Alleviate Climate Change–Related Suffering in the Developing World

As our climate changes and more parts of the world become less habitable, all species that can be negatively affected by climate change have three choices: adapt, migrate or suffer, or possibly die. Some species are capable of moving to more favorable climes and locations while others are not. Humans have long proven their ability to adapt and migrate when times get tough. But over time, we have built so many social, economic, and political barriers around ourselves and

Migration and adaptation are becoming options for only a lucky few.

our nonhuman cousins that migration and adaptation are becoming options for only a lucky few.

My wife constantly reminds me about the number of times we have "migrated" during our marriage. Part of the reason we have been able to move from one state or country to another so easily is luck: We are citizens of a country where people have freedom of movement and passports that allow us to cross most borders, so we can travel to or live in other countries with relative ease. The same is true of citizens of the European Union, Japan, Australia, and residents of a select number of other wealthy countries.

But what about the rest of the world's population, more than 80%? For them different rules apply. Congolese, Sudanese, or Guatemalans cannot easily travel anywhere they want. Numerous political, economic, social, and cultural barriers stand in their way. Any young mainland Chinese graduate student can tell you how hard it is to get a visa to study in the United States. And immigration rules are getting stricter by the day. This is especially true in parts of northern Europe where anti-immigration politicians have made significant electoral gains in recent years. Immigrant-related rioting in France and terrorist attacks in the United Kingdom have soured feelings about immigration there as well (Puget Sound Action Team, 2005).

In recent years, hundreds of millions of people have been displaced by severe weather events.

What does this discussion about human migration have to do with global warming? In recent years, hundreds of millions of people have been displaced by severe weather events, for example, desertification, flooding, and related environmental stresses in countries surrounding the Sahara, Kalahari, and Gobi deserts and in low-lying delta regions. Hurricane Katrina–like events are all too common. Each year, millions of people are temporarily displaced by powerful typhoons and cyclones (Castles, 2002). The Ganges River Delta is one of the most heavily populated places on the planet. Calcutta (Kolkata), the state of West Bengal, and southern Bangladesh are especially susceptible to flooding (Ahmed, Alam, et al., 1999). India's population already tops 1 billion and it is projected to rise to 1.6 billion by 2050 (Brown, 2006). As seas rise and severe weather events proliferate, where are all of these displaced people going to go?

My own wife's hometown, Shanghai, sits atop the flood-prone Yangtze River Delta. While I prefer the relative quiet of Mercer Island, Kela is crazy for Shanghai. She loves the pace of the big city. Shanghai, a major seaport, is especially famous for its seafood. Whenever we visit, Kela cannot resist the endless succession of restaurants that fill every nook of the city. Unfortunately, like many other major cities worldwide, the lifeblood of this metropolis is coal-produced electricity. That, combined with the proliferation of automobiles and other forms of conspicuous consumption, harbors the seeds of the city's own possible destruction.

Also on the list of sea-rise victims are small island nations, mostly in the South Pacific. For the residents of Tuvalu, the effects of global warming are already being felt. The highest point in this small country is about 10 feet above sea level. New Zealand and Australia have already started accepting Tuvalu refugees as the water rises and the landmass of the island shrinks. This tiny nation will more than likely cease to exist as a territorial entity during this century (Byrd, Block, Patterson, and Salzar, 2003). Whole nations swallowed up by the sea—can you imagine what it would be like if your family were in the shoes of these people? What would you do?

Reason 5: Rectify Past Mistakes

The United States and other developed nations bear a heavy historical burden when it comes to suffering brought on by human-induced climate change. Between 1850 and 2000, the United States produced almost 30% of total cumulative global carbon emissions. This is especially notable given the fact that only 2% to 4% of the globe's population called the United States home during the same period. The actual values of the emissions are staggering: 283 tons per person from 1850 to 2000 (81,969 metric tons; WRI, 2006). The historical per capita contribution made by the United Kingdom, Germany, and other developed nations is not far behind.

Relatively few of us are aware of this legacy. And yet the first question many people ask when they learn about this historical responsibility argument is, "Why should I pay for actions taken by past generations?" Well, our present living standard is built on the shoulders of our ancestors. Being born in wealthy nations provides most of us with socioeconomic opportunities that are largely unavailable in much of the developing world. We take access to education, health

our present living standard is built on the shoulders of our ancestors.

care, and material well-being for granted. But for those who have seen the poverty of Mexico City's shantytowns or rural Indian life, the differences are obvious. Citizens of economically deprived and environmentally shattered communities face a triple whammy. First, the fossil fuel–intensive economic model that contributed to our parents', and consequently our own, prosperity is becoming less and less of an option for people in developing countries who still hope to improve their socioeconomic circumstances. Second, most developing countries lack adequate land and other material resources to adapt to intensifying climate-related problems, such as desertification, extreme weather events, rising sea levels, and others. Third, they lack resources and technologies necessary to invest in alternative energy that could help them avoid the destructive consequences wrought by fossil fuel–dependent development.

This question of historical responsibility has played a prominent role in developed-developing world negotiations about sharing the burden in the implementation of the Kyoto Protocol. Developing countries claim that the state members of the Organization of Economically Developed Countries (OECD) have no right to request developing states to commit to mandatory reductions in GHG emissions until they offer some real alternatives to the fossil fuel–intensive development models. As the main emitters of GHGs, the governments and citizens of OECD nations bear a certain amount of responsibility for helping poorer nations alleviate some of the suffering directly caused by human-induced climate change (International Institute for Sustainable Development [IISD], 2002). China, India, and other large developing countries have stated they cannot seriously consider accepting significant mandatory emission limits until developed nations prove they can first reduce their own emissions and provide material, economic, and technological assistance to empower less-developed countries to cut emissions without sacrificing economic growth.

> OECD nations bear some responsibility for helping poorer nations alleviate suffering caused by climate change.

Reason 6: Be Better Stewards

One silver lining behind the climate change crisis is that it is bringing together many formerly ideologically estranged groups. For instance, in the United States environmental activists and evangelical Christians have long engaged in existential battles over a host of social issues, such as abortion, gay marriage, evolution, and so on. However, groups from all sides of the political spectrum are increasingly reaching out to one another in order to save the planet. Traditional left-right political diatribes are increasingly losing their importance in today's debate about climate change. Left-leaning environmentalists realize that fixing the atmosphere requires cooperation from all segments of society.

Groups from all sides of the political spectrum are increasingly reaching out to one another in order to save the planet.

And for their part, evangelical Christians are witnessing a growing movement in their ranks to rediscover environmental ethics. Their term *creation care* reasserts the stewardship message contained in Christian and Jewish religious texts: that the environment and humans are part of God's creation and that their creator expects his followers to take better care of the planet.

One flash point in this debate centers on differing interpretations of the Judeo-Christian creation stories. What role did the Judeo-Christian God want humans to play in the maintenance and use of his creation? Some scholars have come to the conclusion that God gave his followers permission to use and exploit the natural world as they pleased. One passage in particular, Genesis 1:26, has been interpreted to support this contention. One conventional translation states, "Let them have dominion over the fish of the sea, and over the birds of the air, and over the cattle, and over all the earth, and over every creeping thing that creeps upon the earth" (American Revised Standard Version). They believe that this and other statements in Christian texts support the idea that nature is something to be dominated and conquered rather than respected (White, 1967). However, Genesis 2:15 states, "The Lord God took the man and put him in the Garden of Eden to till and keep it" (American Revised Standard Version). The original Hebrew word for "till" refers to an act of work and to an act of service. Service to whom? To the creator. To Jews and Christians, that God created humans is not in question. Nor is God's exhortation that what he created was "good." It is also clear from these and other passages that while humans do have a special role to play in God's plan, they are not the "owners" of creation, God is (Evangelical Environmental Network, 1994). Taken together, these writings reinforce the image of God as creator and humans as stewards, not exploiters (Gottlieb, 2006).

Concern about stewardship is certainly not limited to Judeo-Christian groups. Discussions related to a spiritually motivated moral imperative behind environmental protection have stimulated much ecumenical cooperation among other major faith-based communities (Buddhism, Islam, Hinduism, etc.). Kusumito Peterson (1998) has identified some of the core conclusions of this dialogue. Among other things, major faith-based groups agree that:

- ✓ Nonhuman beings are morally significant in the eyes of God or the cosmic order.

- ✓ The well-being of human and nonhuman beings is inseparably connected.

- ✓ Greed and destruction are condemned. Restraint and protection are commended.

- ✓ Moral norms such as justice, compassion, and reciprocity apply in appropriate ways to human and nonhuman beings.

Reason 7: Beat the "Affluenza" Bug

While overconsumption plagues all industrialized countries, the United States turned it into a high art.

Rampant materialism lies at the root of our current environmental crisis. While overconsumption plagues all industrialized countries, the United States turned it into a high art. James Twitchell (1999) in *Lead Us Into Temptation: The Triumph of American Materialism* chronicles the spread of a dreaded post–World War II disease, *affluenza*. He notes that "hyper-consumption" has given rise to a number of paradoxical cultural orientations. On the one hand, Americans embrace the simplicity, structure, and conservation of their Puritan roots. However, Twitchell notes that paradoxically, "no other culture spends so much time declaring things do not matter while saying 'just charge it.' The country with the highest per capita consumer debt and the greatest number of machine made things is the same country in which Puritan aesthetic principles are most pronounced. . . . on the way to Walden Pond, we pack the sport utility vehicle with the dish antenna, the cell phone, the bread maker, the ashtray, the paddle ball" (p. 2).

As the mania of post–World War II expansion proceeded, little thought was given to the environmental consequences of our material bingeing until it became clear that many of the "wonder" chemicals that made excess consumption possible were literally killing us. This was poignantly expressed in Rachel Carson's environmental wake-up call, *Silent Spring* (1967):

> There was once a town in the heart of America where all life seemed to live in harmony with its surroundings. The town lay in the midst of a checkerboard of prosperous farms, with fields of grain and hillside orchards where, in spring, white clouds of bloom drifted above the green fields. . . . Then a strange blight crept over the area and everything began to change. Some evil spell had settled on the community: mysterious maladies swept the flocks of chickens; the cattle and sheep sickened and died. Everywhere was the shadow of death. . . . there was a strange stillness. . . . a grim specter has crept upon us almost unnoticed. (p. 32)

Carson's poignant prose chronicled the disastrous effects of chemical pesticides, insecticides, fertilizers, and other wonders of modern agriculture on fragile ecosystems. But her prophetic message can just as easily be applied to GHG emissions. Global warming is also a silent killer. Virtually everything we purchase—food, toys, bottled water, autos, ice cream—requires fossil fuels to produce, transport, and store. The effects of our shopping malady appear harmless enough, but each new purchase can exacerbate our climate crisis.

> Virtually everything we purchase . . . requires fossil fuels to produce, transport, and store.

Reason 8: Save the Commons

Also contributing to mounting GHG emissions is that government regulators and private markets often greatly undervalue the social and economic consequences of production, distribution, marketing, or waste disposal in the prices of goods and services (Goodland and Ledee, 1987). Most governments have lax to nonexistent carbon dioxide emissions regulations, so producers and end users spew it into the atmosphere with abandon, with few or no consequences to the polluter. This is an example of what Garret Hardin and like-minded thinkers call the "tragedy of the commons" (Hardin, 1968). Unlike private property, our atmosphere is a public resource. Everyone has access to it. If no deterrent exists to limit its

> If no deterrent exists to limit the atmosphere's use, individuals and firms are naturally inclined to overexploit it.

use, individuals and firms are naturally inclined to overexploit it, which may degrade it to the point where it is no longer valuable to anyone (Brown, 2005).

Affluenza and the tragedy of the commons should have great relevance to anyone who is concerned about the personal implications of overconsumption. As moral actors, we should not just wait for markets or governments to accurately take into account the true costs of Wal-Mart shopping or family trips to Bermuda in prices for goods and services. We need to acknowledge that using our atmosphere is never free. Each of us has a responsibility to use public goods in a sustainable way. Minimizing use offers the best path for doing this. Second, if we must use public goods (e.g., spew carbon dioxide into the atmosphere) and neither governments nor markets force us to pay extra for the privilege, we should consider voluntarily giving something back to society, such as time or money, to make up for our actions. For example, if you need to fly from New York City to London for work, you or your employer can purchase "carbon offsets" that reduce your GHG impact in an amount equivalent to the emissions produced during your trip. A *carbon offset* is a payment that we make to someone else to reduce GHG emissions by a specified amount (see chapters 7 and 8 for more information on carbon offsets). The offsets can then be used to make investments in projects aimed at reducing emissions, such as wind farms or solar collectors (Point Carbon, 2007).

> Each of us has a responsibility to use public goods in a sustainable way.

Reason 9: Save Money

> Going on a Climate Diet is almost certain to save you lots of money.

Let's get one thing clear: Going on a Climate Diet is almost certain to save you lots of money—either immediately or over time. As a money-deprived college professor, I can speak from personal experience. One of my colleagues was complaining about having to spend more than $70 filling up his pickup truck's gas tank. For those of you who live in Japan or France, that might sound like a bargain. But Americans still long for the days of cheap energy. Traveling a similar distance in a Honda Civic can cost one-third the price of making the same journey in an SUV. Three words describe the driving philosophy behind the Climate Diet: conserve, conserve, conserve. Chapters 3 through 7 are filled with dozens of low-cost, high-impact lifestyle changes you can make that save both money and the atmosphere. If you follow my recommendations, you will cut your energy bill by up to $7,600 per year at 2006–2007 prices, or even more if you live in Europe, Australia, or Japan.

Reason 10: Save Nature for Its Own Sake

We have many motivations behind our desire to protect the climate. Some of us do it to try to placate a higher being, while others do it to serve themselves. Human-centered arguments form the basis of modern environmentalism. However, many ecocentrist thinkers believe that nature has innate value above and beyond our own species-centric need to use and enjoy it. In other words, they believe that we, as moral actors and cohabitants of this tiny planet, should protect nature for nature's sake.

In 1949 naturalist Aldo Leopold wrote a thin little book titled *A Sand County Almanac: And Sketches Here and There*. Leopold rejected the notion expressed by early 20th-century conservationists that nature's primary purpose is to serve human aesthetic and material needs. Rather, he believed we should recognize that *Homo sapiens* is just one of the millions of species that inhabit this planet and that it is in our own self-interest and morally correct to live in harmony with the biosphere. Leopold's environmental ethic is simple. He wrote: "A thing is right when it tends to preserve the integrity, stability and beauty of the biotic community. It is wrong when it tends otherwise" (p. 238). He continues, "All ethics so far evolved rest upon a single premise: that the individual is a member of a community of interdependent parts. His instincts prompt him to compete for his place in that community, but his ethics prompt him also to cooperate. . . . the land ethic simply enlarges the boundaries of the community to include soils, waters, plants and animals, or collectively: the land" (p. 239).

For ecocentrists, Leopold's land ethic has a profound implication. They assert that another cause of the current climate crisis is our unwillingness to acknowledge the breadth, intricacy, and interconnectedness of the global biosphere. Recent attempted human domination of the biosphere is but a tiny blip in the eons-long history of Mother Earth. Over time, countless species have come and gone.

One of the cruel truths of evolution is that the very circumstances that encourage species to thrive and multiply often sow the seeds of their own destruction.

Intelligence and free agency have allowed humanity to spread its influence over every nook and cranny of the Earth. But the very traits that allow humans to establish their hegemony are altering the paper-thin shroud that blankets our planet and destabilizing the biotic community that we depend on for our own survival (Lovelock, 2006).

Whether you believe in science, God, Mother Nature, or all of the above, there is no denying that the small planet we live on is immensely beautiful. Dense coniferous canopies of pine and spruce still cover parts of the Cascade Range and the western Rocky Mountains. There is nothing more relaxing than walking inside these immense groves. Ferns blanket the ground. Green, yellow, and olive-colored mosses and lichens coat every tree and rock. Spiders weave silvery strands among the undergrowth. Fallen timbers, like wet nurses, bring new life to the forest. Pine needles and centuries-old root systems snap and bellow underfoot. The sublime sound of trees rustling in the wind is ever present. Douglas squirrels chirp merrily as they go about their work. The floor of this magnificent canopy is full of shadows and darkness. But if you look up, a whole new world awaits. Slender spires reach gracefully toward the sun. An entirely different ecosystem governs these heights. Creation does indeed offer up an unending barrage of delights.

Each one of us has our own story to tell about a place that has touched our souls. For some, desert landscapes make the heart palpitate. Others are enamored of the dark hues of fog passing over a Scottish loch in winter. But the real source of this natural bounty is its own intricacy, its innate value as a whole. How can we expect our children to value the living world around us if we do not value it ourselves through our own actions? Shouldn't our children be provided the same opportunities to connect with the natural world that we have enjoyed?

How can we expect our children to value the living world if we do not value it ourselves through our own actions?

Ten reasons. Pick any one you want. Mother Earth does not care what motivates you to reduce your climate footprint. All the debate in the world about the roots of our environmental crisis will not solve the problem. The only thing that matters to her is action. Now, turn the page to chapter 3. Let's gets started on our Climate Diet!

Going for the Gold: The Nuts and Volts of Climate Diet Success

3

I hope by now you are convinced that climate change is a real and present danger and that you and your family should explore strategies to confront this threat to our future. Now comes the exciting part: turning good wishes into concrete actions. Chapters 3–8 provide detailed guidance on how we can set goals and make effective climate dieting decisions that can be tailored to fit almost any lifestyle.

This chapter includes three major sections. First of all, before we begin our quest for the Gold we should spend a few minutes learning more about how greenhouse emissions are created and measured so we can better understand how our actions affect the atmosphere. It is much easier than you might think. Second, I will introduce my "zones to success," a strategy we can use to define and evaluate the climate effects of our lifestyles room by room at home, when shopping, eating, and on the road. Third, I will present three diet plans we can use to achieve Climate Diet success: the Shortest-Cut Diet Plan, the Shortcut Diet plan, and the Full Home Audit and Comprehensive Diet Plan.

Energy and Carbon Dioxide: The Basics

OK, I 'fess up. I am pushing 19–20 pounds over my wedding-day weight. But for me to put together a plan to lose that flab, I need to know which foods and activities I should stay away from to get back into shape. Likewise, if we are really going to develop a strategy to cut our climate impact, we need to know more about how specific actions, such as changing a lightbulb, can affect our "carbon dioxide weight." We need to find a way to count our calories when it comes to energy use. Enter the Climate Diet.

Most of us already know that a calorie is a unit of energy. Our food-based calories come in many forms, and different calorie sources have varying effects on our bodies. Nutrition labels give us a breakdown of where these calories come from, such as fats, carbohydrates, or proteins.

In the natural sciences, a number of other terms are used to describe energy. Electricity is usually measured in watts (1,000 watts used for 1 hour = 1 kilowatt hour [kWh]), while energy derived from the burning of natural gas or oil is measured in British thermal units (Btu; 100,000 Btu = 1 therm). One Btu is the amount of heat needed

> We need to find a way to count our calories when it comes to energy use.

to increase the temperature of one pound of water by $1°F$ ($0.6°C$) Because these are all standard units of energy—calories, Btu, and watts—they are all convertible from one to the other. For instance, if you wanted to, you could compute how many equivalent watts your body uses every day.

> The electricity we use comes from a mix of renewable and nonrenewable sources. Each community is different.

The electricity we use comes from a mix of renewable and nonrenewable sources. Each community is different. In Washington state, an above-average amount of energy is generated by large hydroelectric dams, where the force of flowing water turns giant turbines, thus generating power. Solar power generation is virtually GHG-free. On the other hand, in Appalachia or Beijing, soft coal is the primary fuel of choice. Since coal briquettes are little more than big chunks of carbon, burning them generates lots of carbon dioxide. Carbon dioxide calculations used in this book are based on average country/state/provincial mixes. The default used in our Climate Diet example is from the United States (see Appendices C and D for carbon dioxide equivalent electricity emissions coefficients for your country/state/province). So, your family's actual GHG emissions will vary depending on where you reside.

It should be noted that two phrases are used to describe GHGs in this book. Carbon dioxide refers to carbon dioxide emissions only. Carbon dioxide equivalent (or CO_2e) refers to carbon dioxide as well as the carbon dioxide equivalent effects (when available) of other GHGs. The carbon dioxide equivalent value is determined by adding up the relative contribution of different gases as measured in carbon dioxide units ($CO_2 + CH_4 + N_2O$). Carbon dioxide equivalent values are mainly used in the food and waste zones described in chapter 6. Each of these gases has a different "global warming potential." For instance, 1 metric ton of methane has an effect equivalent to 21 metric tons of carbon dioxide.

Candy Versus Carrots: Counting Carbon "Calories"

Have you ever wondered how much carbon dioxide is emitted by specific actions, such as turning on a lightbulb or heating your house or apartment for a month?

For starters, let's examine the energy use, carbon dioxide emissions, and electricity cost for two types of lightbulbs. If you have been in the market for a lightbulb lately, you are probably aware that compact fluorescent lightbulbs (CFLs) are now widely available. These bulbs emit almost the same amount of light as regular incandescent bulbs but use about 70% to 75% less electricity. The average 100 watt incandescent lightbulb expends 100 watts, or 1 kWh (1,000 watts) over the course of 10 hours. In contrast, the CFL uses about 23 to 29 watts (depending on the brand) to produce almost the same amount of light. Why such a big difference? Incandescent bulbs are really inefficient. Only about 10% of the electricity they use actually ends up producing light. The rest dissipates in the form of heat. We can use the simple formula in Table 3.1 to figure out the environmental and financial impacts of changing to a CFL.

Next, you can calculate the yearly electricity cost difference by multiplying the total kWh for each bulb by the cost you pay per kWh. In September 2007, the U.S. national retail average cost per kWh was 10.65 cents see Appendices C and D for average electricity costs in your country/state/province (EIA, 2007). The average yearly electricity cost for the incandescent bulb is $18.69 versus $5.42 for the CFL. Yes, it is true that CFLs often cost more than "regular" ones. But they more than pay for themselves over time. CFLs also typically last longer, which accrues added savings.

Table 3.1 **Lightbulb Example**

	Incandescent	Compact Fluorescent
Watts	100	29
Hours used per day (U.S. national average)	5	5
Days used per year (excludes vacation time)	351	351
Total Wh/year	175,000	50,895
Total kWh/year	175.5	50.895

Formula used for total kWh/year:

$$\frac{\text{(Watts) x (hours used per day) x (days used per year)}}{1000} = \text{kWh per year}$$

Table 3.2 Summary of the Information You Need for Your Climate Diet

Electricity (U.S. average)	1.363 lb (0.62 kg) CO_2 per kWh (EPA, 2007a)
Natural Gas	11.68 lb (5.3 kg) CO_2 per therm (EPA, 2007b)
Heating Oil	16.10 lb (7.3 kg) CO_2 per therm (EPA, 2007b)
Gasoline	20 lb (9.08 kg) CO_2 per gallon (EPA, 2007c)

Note: Emissions are for CO_2 only.

Table 3.3 Mercer Island Example

Energy Values	Month (July)	Conversion Value	Total CO_2
kWh	273	1.363 lb (0.62 kg)	372 lb (169 kg)
Therm	8.22	11.68 lb (5.3 kg)	96 lb (43.6 kg)
Total			468 lb (212.5 kg)

Using less electricity is going to drastically reduce our electricity bill.

At this point, we know that using less electricity is going to drastically reduce our electricity bill. But what about our climate impact? Table 3.2 presents the GHG emissions of different types of fuels.

Now, let's go back to our lightbulb example. In the United States, generating 1 kWh of electricity generates about 1.363 lb (0.62 kg) of carbon dioxide. So, if we multiply the total kWh for each bulb by 1.363 lb (0.62 kg) we can find the comparative carbon dioxide emissions for the two bulbs. The incandescent bulb emits 239 lb (108.5 kg) of carbon dioxide (175.5 kWh × 1.363 lb) while the CFL emits 69.4 lb (31.5 kg) of carbon dioxide (50.895 kWh × 1.363 lb).

So, based on this one example, changing to a CFL reduces GHG emissions and electricity costs by more than 70%. You just won yourself a Silver Medal! See, that wasn't so hard, was it?

You can use this same information to establish a baseline to evaluate how future lifestyle changes influence your overall energy use and associated emissions. Just take a look at your monthly utility bill. The total number of kWh you use (or Btu or therms for oil or natural gas heating) should be printed on your bill (note: Climate Diet table values do not include all taxes). To find your total environmental impact, just multiply your monthly energy-use amounts and their respective carbon dioxide values for various fuel types listed in Table 3.2 and total up the emissions from each fuel type.

Let's look at another example. Table 3.3 measures the energy and emissions of the Harrington residence (my home on Mercer Island) in July 2006. Our family used 273 kWh of electricity and more than 8 Btu of natural gas, mostly for cooking and heating water.

In total, our family generated 468 lb (212.5 kg) of carbon dioxide from energy-related household activities. That is almost the same weight as one sumo wrestler. Now, if you multiply that by 12 months, the number gets really big. All of those sumo stars are going to eat you out of house and home if you don't do something fast!

To recap, in most cases figuring out your climate impact requires three pieces of information: fuel used, amount of time used (or distance traveled) to use that fuel, and the associated carbon dioxide equivalent factor. The household example allows us to calculate our total monthly electricity and heating use and its associated emissions. You can use your own household-specific information to replicate the lightbulb or Mercer Island example. For a more accurate assessment for your own community, refer to Table 3.4, which provides cost and GHG factor data for selected countries. If your country is not listed, go to Appendices C and D for a more complete list. In effect, we just "weighed" ourselves, similar to what we do when we step on the scale in the morning.

Zones to Success

During the past few years, millions of households went on a home improvement tear. Everyone seemed to be in the process of remodeling their domiciles, didn't they? Well, whenever we engage in a remodeling project, we usually plan our changes room by room. However, at the same time, we are also aware of how changes in one room may be linked to other parts of our home and our lifestyle. The Climate Diet takes a similar room-by-room approach. But instead of the word *room*, we will use the term *zone* to differentiate among parts of our fossil fuel–using

Table 3.4 Sample GHG Factor and Electricity Cost Data for Selected Countries

Country	GHG Factor (lb)	Cost ($/kWh)
Australia	1.72	0.0985
Canada	0.48	0.0676
Germany	1.12	0.2124
South Korea	0.99	0.1034
United States	1.363	0.1065
United Kingdom	1.02	0.2205

Source: International Energy Agency (2006, 2007), *Key World Energy Statistics: 2006,* 2007 IEA, Paris; IEA (2005) *CO$_2$ Emissions From Fuel Consumption: 1971–2003,* IEA, Paris.

Zones can include rooms, areas, or actions that have an impact on the atmosphere.

lives. Zones can include rooms, areas, or actions that have an impact on the atmosphere. But rather than replacing one perfectly good fridge with a shiny new one, as is usually the case in a kitchen makeover, our ultimate remodeling goal is to get a better idea of where we are in terms of our current climate impact and how specific conserving lifestyle changes can reduce it.

The Climate Diet uses a model household to illustrate the effect of lifestyle changes on our carbon dioxide weight. Our model is not located in a particular country but is designed to apply to a midlatitude temperate zone (40 degrees north or south, Boston, for example) where direct household carbon dioxide emissions hover between 15,000 and 20,000 lb (6,810 kg to 9,080 kg) per capita, or roughly one-half of per capita emissions derived from all sources (according to the IEA's *Key World Energy Statistics* (2006), total per capita emissions from all sources were 19.73 metric tons in the United States, 17.53 in Australia, and 17.24 in Canada). Our model household also reflects typical housing stock available in these countries/latitudes. Because of its comparative nature, the model does not provide precise carbon dioxide estimates for each and every locale, but it does provide a useful reference point we can use to design our own Climate Diet. The following is a list of zones and related assumptions based on our model house.

Climate Diet Zones

Home interior zones are based on a more than 20-year-old, 2,000-square-foot (sq ft; 186 square meters [sq m]), three-bedroom, two-bath, single detached house with a yard. Interior zones include a living/dining room zone, kitchen zone, bedroom 1/kids' room zone, bedroom 2/master suite zone, bedroom 3/home office zone, bathrooms zone, and a laundry/utility zone (described in detail in chapter 4). The heating zone and air-conditioning zone are discussed in chapter 5.

The **yard zone** includes external lighting, external cooking apparatuses, pools/saunas, lawn mowers, weed trimmers, and so on, as well as gardening practices (detailed in chapter 5).

The **food and waste zone** includes carbon dioxide equivalent impacts for consumption of selected food items, waste, and recycling (detailed in chapter 6).

The **transportation zone** measures comparative carbon dioxide impacts for different modes of transportation by distance traveled (detailed in chapter 7).

Use the sample worksheets in Appendix B to create **other zones**. The Climate Diet provides plenty of opportunities for customization. You can download all the worksheets for the model house zones at www.climatediet.com/tables.asp.

Three Paths to a Cooler Climate

You can go on a Climate Diet in one of three ways:

1   Shortest-Cut Diet Plan

2   Shortcut Diet Plan

3   Full Home Audit and Comprehensive Diet Plan

Shortest-Cut Diet Plan

With this plan, just read chapters 3 through 8 and replicate the lifestyle changes suggested for our model house. Want to do a complete makeover, or just concentrate on some trouble spots? Use my handy outlines at the beginning of each chapter to quickly find the advice and information you are looking for. Suggestions summarized in the Tips Summary section at the end of each chapter will reduce your carbon footprint. You may also want to check your monthly energy bills to establish a baseline for making future comparisons. Compare like months to track how much money you are saving.

Suggestion summarized in the Tips Summary section at the end of each chapter will reduce your carbon footprint.

Shortcut Diet Plan

Under this plan, you use one year of electricity/heating bills to establish a baseline for future comparisons. Figure out your monthly energy use on a month-by-month basis from January to December. Use the formula on p. 33 to calculate your electricity use. Multiply your total kWh for each month by the GHG conversion factor (hereafter referred to as the GHG factor) provided in Table 3.2 on p. 34 to find your carbon output. To find the climate effect of heating, multiply the unit values from your monthly heating bill by the appropriate GHG factor (like in the Mercer Island example). You can find more detailed instructions on how to use these values in Appendix B, "Sample Climate Diet Worksheet." Make suggested lifestyle changes in the Tips Summary section of each chapter and then monitor your bills on a monthly basis comparing month to like month—January to January, February to February—and see what sort of reductions in energy and carbon dioxide you have achieved, and then see if you can improve a bit each month. Also, read the remaining chapters including those on shopping and eating (chapter 6) and transportation (chapter 7) and implement all the tips for reducing your climate impact.

Full Home Audit and Comprehensive Diet Plan

For this plan we precisely calculate how much energy is used in various rooms and for different appliances and then use this information to plan specific changes to reduce your carbon footprint and to track this change. The model house example provides a working illustration of exactly how this can be done. Commonly used items and their associated energy use and carbon dioxide output are calculated for each room. The core of this plan is the worksheet (which was used for all the model house zone calculations) provided in Appendix B and in the downloadable tables (www.climatediet.com/tables.asp). In the following chapters, you will learn how to use the worksheet and develop a detailed profile of your energy usage and carbon footprint in the home, yard, and on the road. Detailed energy use data for dozens of products are provided in Appendix E. You will also find plenty of useful tips for reducing your climate impact in the way you shop and what you choose to eat.

How much did cutting down on watching TV, eating beef, or automobile commuting affect your overall climate impact? How much "weight" did you lose? Two summary tables in chapter 9 allow you to tally your results so you can see how much total carbon and money you have already saved and where you can improve even more.

If you do not have the time or desire to fully implement the Full Home Audit and Comprehensive Diet Plan, you may want to mix and match the shortcut plans. You can hone in on one room or two. Or you may want to leave the interior as is and just focus on the yard. If environmentally friendly transportation is your passion, jump to chapter 7 and check out the corresponding transportation zone worksheet. Or cut back on your eating and shopping footprint by checking out the food zone and waste zone discussion and corresponding worksheets in chapter 6.

Choices, Choices, Choices

I hope you will agree that the Climate Diet can be used almost anywhere and fits almost any lifestyle. I should note that *cost savings only apply to energy costs*. Other factors, such as original purchase price or other life cycle costs, are not included. Product and service costs vary too widely for them to be covered in this comparative cross-national model. You will need to evaluate your own circumstances before deciding if purchasing more efficient products or services makes sense for your family (but most suggestions require little or no additional investment).

Finally, some of you may be thinking, "This is a great approach. But I don't like numbers." No problem. Just like regular food diets, you do not have to count every calorie or weigh every portion in order to cut your climate impact. If that's your case, then the Shortest-Cut Diet Plan (which requires no calculations) is just what you are looking for. The real key to successful climate dieting is developing an understanding of which types of lifestyle changes will bring the biggest (and most cost-effective) reductions. Whatever approach you take, the Climate Diet will reduce your family's production of GHGs. And that is healthy weight loss.

Less Is More: Creating a Climate Diet Home

4

During the first few years of the 21st century, many regions of the world were gripped by a home-building boom. Shanghai added 100 new skyscrapers to the city's skyline each year. Seemingly insatiable demand drove property prices in central London through the stratosphere. Along the Spanish Riviera, McMansions popped up like daisies. Home ownership is viewed by many to be the cornerstone of financial and personal independence. Generous government incentives, such as mortgage interest deductions and other tax breaks, often fueled this building frenzy.

North Americans were also eager participants in this home-buying binge. New building starts reached levels not seen in decades. And not only were they buying more condos, town houses, and houses, but their little palaces were bigger and fancier than ever. Remodeling continues to be a popular pastime. For the frenzied homeowners who are working on fixer-uppers, weekly visits to the local home improvement store are a must. Sunday pilgrimages to these big-box cathedrals of consumption are fast supplanting traditional church attendance.

Home ownership also increasingly means not only possessing bricks and mortar, but also meticulously preserving the land around the edifice. Weekend warriors derive great satisfaction from maintaining their yards just so—spending hours each week caring for their beautiful green lawns, perfectly kept gardens, and painstakingly pruned shrubbery. Also in recent years the boundary between inside and outside has become increasingly blurred as we expand our dominions outward—installing new patios, swimming pools, and other accoutrements to make our yards and balconies more comfortable and useful.

Different Homes: Different Climate Outcomes

Given the impact that our home life has on the climate, it is fitting that we begin our discussion about climate dieting strategies here. You may not know it, but the typical detached suburban house is a little GHG factory. Among household energy-use activities (not including transportation), heating and cooling typically leads the way, followed by

The typical detached suburban house is a little GHG factory.

electrical appliances, lighting, and water heating (U.S. Department of Energy, 2007).

One thing we need to establish from the start is that no two houses, or families, are alike. Even tract houses that look identical from the outside may have different environmental impacts, as each household has its own unique living style. However, certain common factors influence each family's climate impact. Home size and age figure among the most important. My family's "little slice of heaven" was built in 1959 and is approximately 2,000 sq ft (186 sq m). Our house is slightly larger than other structures built during that period. However, over the years home girth in the United States and most other developed countries has edged higher; new U.S. homes now average more than 2,500 sq ft (232 sq m).

Smaller domiciles have a number of things going for them. They generally contain fewer power outlets, water faucets, toilets, and showers. They require less furniture and fewer electronic gadgets, such as televisions, refrigerators, and so on. Also, their smaller volume means less air to heat and cool. On the other hand, older structures are generally less well insulated and often have older and less-efficient appliances, water heaters, and air conditioners.

Climate, geography, and energy availability also influence household emissions. The further away your average outdoor temperature is from 72° F (22° C), which is the typical indoor temperature Americans are most accustomed to, the more GHG you are likely to produce. This *magic* temperature has nothing to do with health or necessity. When we lived in Tokyo (where winter temperatures are similar to those of the Seattle area) neither we nor our neighbors used our heaters during the day and suffered no negative health effects. Seventy-two degrees Fahrenheit (22° C) is simply what Americans are used to. Seattleites run their heaters more than six months a year, but cooler summers mean that few people own central air conditioners. But if you live in Miami your air conditioner gets a real workout: 3,931 hours/year (Energy Star, 2006). Also, other factors such as vegetation and land use practices can affect indoor temperatures. If you live in a forest (as we do on Mercer Island) access to sunlight may be limited, thus alleviating the need for air-conditioning, but sun-blocking trees may increase winter heating demands. But in your community, you may want to plant some trees around your house to protect it from

Certain common factors influence each family's climate impact. Home size and age figure among the most important.

the scorching summer sun. Finally, carbon dioxide emissions from the combustion of different fuels vary considerably. Natural gas generates about one-third fewer emissions than heating oil (assuming equivalent efficiency of household heating systems). Also, GHG emissions from electricity generation vary.

Finally, emissions are affected by the length of time appliances and other items are used. The average working American receives about two weeks of vacation time per year. This may sound a bit shocking if you live in parts of Europe where paid holidays can last six weeks or longer. This book is probably not the place to debate the benefits and costs (are there any?) of more vacation time. However, it does have an effect on our Climate Diet. Our model home calculations assume that readers are stuck at home 351 days a year.

> Natural gas generates about one-third fewer emissions than heating oil.

Where Should You Begin? The Bedrooms

Where should you begin your quest for a healthier climate? My answer to this question is, simply, wherever you want. Is there a part of the house you want to update? Are you itching to improve the lighting in your favorite reading spot? Or do you have a growing daughter who constantly complains about how "boring" her room is? Fortunately, the Climate Diet is so flexible you can start anywhere without losing a beat.

Coincidentally, I just happen to have a daughter who really does want a room makeover. So, let's start with Kela's room in our model house. We already have all the tools we need to get started. If you are following the Shortest-Cut Diet Plan, just follow our discussion and make recommended changes as appropriate. If you are a Full Home Audit and Comprehensive Diet Plan dieter, download the zone worksheet tables from www.climatediet.com/tables.asp and enter your energy-use values in the red boxes for each room. Percentage GHG reductions will be automatically tallied (and medals conferred) by zone.

In our case, Kela's bedroom is packed with stuff—too much stuff. Fortunately, only a few items use electricity: one table lamp (60 watts), a ceiling fan (75 watts) with a light fixture (150 watts), and a portable stereo (15 watts). If you plan a lifestyle change, write down the new items and the corresponding values for time used and emissions. In this example, activities in Kela's room use around 425 kWh per year and

Table 4.1 Bedroom 1/Kid's Room

Item/Service	Current—Where You Are			Future—Where You Want to Be			
	kWh/yr	CO_2/yr (lb)	CO_2 (kg)	kWh/yr	CO_2/yr (lb)	CO_2/yr (kg)	CO_2 Cut
Bedroom 1 Zone							
Ceiling fan	79.0	107.6	48.8	63.2	86.1	39.1	20%
Stereo (desk)	15.8	21.5	9.8	15.8	21.5	9.8	0%
Electric air conditioner	35.1	47.8	21.7	35.1	47.8	21.7	0%
Items subtotal	129.9	177.0	80.3	114.1	155.5	70.5	12%
Lighting Sheet							
Incandescent Watts (W)							
60 W	84.2	114.8	52.1	21.1	28.7	13.0	75%
150 W	210.6	287.0	130.2	53.4	72.7	33.0	75%
Lighting Subtotal	294.8	401.9	182.3	74.4	101.4	46.0	75%
Total	424.7	578.9	262.6	188.5	256.9	116.5	56%
Quick Cost Comparison							
$ Old Cost		45.23		$/kWh	0.1065		
$ New Cost		20.07					
$ Savings		25.16					

Note: Remember that you can download and customize your own zone sheets from www.climatediet. com/tables.asp. All zone table values are calculated using Microsoft Excel and are recorded to five decimal places.

Switching to an efficient ceiling fan can save you money.

generate 579 lb (262.6 kg) of carbon dioxide. A quick look at the zone worksheet reveals that changing a few lightbulbs to CFL equivalents and getting a more efficient ceiling fan can cut her emissions by 56% to about 257 lb (116.5 kg) of carbon dioxide. Also, switching to an efficient ceiling fan can save you money by helping to distribute air around the house evenly and can reduce or eliminate the need for air-conditioning.

Making the suggested changes to your Kid's Room will reduce your carbon dioxide emissions by 56% (322 lb/146 kg), cut your electric bill by $25, and earn you a Silver Medal.

Bedroom 2 has a few more creature comforts. We could call this

Table 4.2 Bedroom 2/Master Suite

Item/Service	Current—Where You Are			Future—Where You Want to Be			
	kWh/yr	CO$_2$/yr (lb)	CO$_2$/yr (kg)	kWh/yr	CO$_2$/yr (lb)	CO$_2$/yr (kg)	CO$_2$ Cut
Bedroom 2 Zone							
Ceiling fan	79.0	107.6	48.8	79.0	107.6	48.8	0%
Clock	17.5	23.9	10.8	17.5	23.9	10.8	0%
DVD	2.0	2.7	1.2	2.0	2.7	1.2	0%
Stereo (desk)	15.8	21.5	9.8	15.8	21.5	9.8	0%
TV 27 in	158.7	216.2	98.1	158.7	216.2	98.1	0%
Video game console	14.0	19.1	8.7	14.0	19.1	8.7	0%
Electric air cleaner	35.1	47.8	21.7	35.1	47.8	21.7	0%
Portable heater	480.0	654.2	296.8	0.0	0.0	0.0	100%
Electric blanket	0.0	0.0	0.0	28.8	39.3	17.8	-100%
Items Subtotal	**802.1**	**1,093.2**	**495.9**	**350.9**	**478.2**	**216.9**	**56%**
Lighting Sheet							
60 W	84.2	114.8	52.1	21.1	28.7	13.0	75%
100 W	561.6	765.5	347.2	162.9	222.0	100.7	71%
150 W	210.6	287.0	130.2	53.4	72.7	33.0	75%
Lighting Subtotal	**856.4**	**1,167.3**	**529.5**	**237.4**	**323.4**	**146.7**	**72%**
Total	**1,658.5**	**2,260.6**	**1,025.4**	**588.3**	**801.7**	**363.6**	**65%**
Quick Cost Comparison							
$ Old Cost		176.63		$/kWh	0.1065		
$ New Cost		62.65					
$ Savings		113.98					

our master suite, such as it may be in a 20- to 30-year-old 2,000 sq ft house. Beyond lighting, one of the biggest power users is the ubiquitous television set. Over the years, television use and ownership has continued to increase worldwide. Fortunately, these information appliances are much more efficient than they used to be. In 2006 liquid crystal display (LCD) sets were already overtaking their cathode-ray tube (CRT) ancestors in the computer area. In a few years, we may be hard pressed to find any CRT screens on store shelves (Cubarrubia, 2006).

Many of you may be thinking that this Climate Diet thing looks like a good excuse to run out to your local appliance store to pick up a new TV set. Should you spend hundreds of dollars for a new set to save 10–20 watts in energy? Will you watch TV even more than you already do? Is that a good idea? It makes much more sense just to buy a few new CFLs. Before making any new purchase, it is important to remember that the manufacturing, distribution, and later disposal of products (often referred to as *life cycle costs*) also generate GHG emissions. So if your already existing appliance is in perfectly good working order, it is often better to forgo replacing it until its useful life has ended. If you really want instant gratification, rather than buying a new feel-good gadget, just cut back on your use a bit and watch your energy bill drop.

> Manufacturing, distribution, and later disposal of products also generate GHG emissions.

For the model home master bedroom, I also suggest one other possible change. This room is drafty at night so its occupants supplement their central heater with a space heater. Portable space heaters use lots of energy. If you feel chilly at night an electric blanket will work just as well.

Making these few changes to bedroom 2 will cut your carbon dioxide emissions by 65%, save around $114 in energy costs, and earn you a Silver Medal.

The Home Office

Our model home is well endowed with all the information accoutrements that bind us to the working world. Like TVs, power consumption for electronic office products has dropped significantly but in ways that might not be immediately obvious. Let's look at an example. There is not much variation in energy use between an Energy Star–rated and a nonrated 19-inch LCD monitor when they are in "on" mode. This is also true for most copiers, fax machines, and printers. Energy savings really accrue when these devices are in standby or sleep mode. In this worksheet, energy values for these products have been adjusted to take this difference into account. Did you know that a non-Energy Star copier can use almost as much energy in standby

Table 4.3 **Bedroom 3/Home Office**

Item/Service	Current—Where You Are			Future—Where You Want to Be			
	kWh/yr	CO_2/yr (lb)	CO_2 (kg)	kWh/yr	CO_2/yr (lb)	CO_2/yr (kg)	CO_2 Cut
Bedroom 3 Office Zone							
Portable fan	31.6	43.1	19.5	31.6	43.1	19.5	0%
Clock	17.5	23.9	10.8	17.5	23.9	10.8	0%
DVD	2.0	2.7	1.2	2.0	2.7	1.2	0%
Stereo (desk)	15.8	21.5	9.8	15.8	21.5	9.8	0%
Computer	44.8	61.0	27.7	44.8	61.0	27.7	0%
Printer	22.5	30.7	13.9	9.0	12.2	5.5	60%
Electric air cleaner	35.1	47.8	21.7	35.1	47.8	21.7	0%
Fax	38.6	52.7	23.9	38.6	52.7	23.9	0%
Copier	90.1	122.8	55.7	0.0	0.0	0.0	100%
LCD 19 in	55.5	75.7	34.3	11.6	15.8	7.2	79%
Items Subtotal	**353.6**	**481.9**	**218.6**	**206.0**	**280.8**	**127.4**	**42%**
Lighting Sheet							
Incandescent Watts (W)							
60 W (2)	168.5	229.6	104.2	42.1	57.4	26.0	75%
100 W (3)	421.2	574.1	260.4	122.1	166.5	75.5	71%
Lighting Subtotal	**589.7**	**803.7**	**364.6**	**164.3**	**223.9**	**101.6**	**72%**
Total office	**943.3**	**1,285.7**	**583.2**	**370.3**	**504.7**	**228.9**	**61%**
Quick Cost Comparison							
$ Old Cost		100.46		$/kWh	0.1065		
$ New Cost		39.44					
$ Savings		61.02					

mode as it does in the "on" mode? The Energy Star and a nonrated 0- to 10-page low-speed copier use 115 watts in "on" mode. However, in standby mode the Energy Star model uses 34 watts versus 110 watts for the nonrated model.

Here are some other characteristics of Energy Star–rated products:

✓ Computers automatically power down to 30 watts or less when not in use.

✓ Scanners go into sleep mode after 15 minutes of nonuse.

✓ Printers power down to 15 watts to 45 watts.

✓ Monitors power down to 30 watts or less when not in use. (Natural Resources Canada [NRC], 2006)

Many products power down in two stages, eventually transitioning into a "deep sleep" mode that saves even more energy. Most Energy Star and equivalently rated small electric appliances have this feature. However, differences in standby power use tend to be much larger for office equipment than for other product categories. The only downside to this power-down process is that it takes time for machines to power back up so they can be used again (Energy Star, 2006).

The sad part of this story is that it costs manufacturers almost nothing to adjust their machines to power down when not in use, but these machines are not widely available. However, even when they are, we more often than not buy the nonrated products.

> There is a quick and easy solution to the standby power problem. Just unplug your machines at the source.

Of course, there is a quick and easy solution to the standby power problem. Just turn off or unplug your machines at the source. Use a power strip or a mains wall or socket switch that you can use to shut off current to whatever is plugged into it. Doing this will save you the trouble of spending hundreds of dollars for products whose main claim to fame is that they remember to turn themselves off when they are not being used.

Unfortunately, the reality is that despite our best intentions, we often do forget to power down energy-hungry office products. Therefore, it may make sense to purchase a few key items (to replace those that are near the end of their useful lives) to reduce our carbon emissions (and increase your productivity). Our model house illustrates the benefits of purchasing a more efficient LCD monitor and printer. Another thing you might want to consider is cutting that home copier out of your life. Most of us love the idea that we can make a copy of anything anytime, but home copiers rarely get used enough to justify their cost. They just sit there, day in and day out, sucking up electricity. I almost guarantee you that you will also end up making fewer copies, which has other environmental benefits.

> Home copiers rarely get used enough to justify their cost.

Making the suggested changes and converting all lightbulbs to CFLs will cut your carbon dioxide emissions 61% (781 lb/354 kg), your electric bill by $61, and win you another Silver Medal.

The Living/Dining Room

In recent years, there has been a sea change in the way many of us use our living/dining areas. In an earlier era, living and dining rooms were reserved for formal activities like parties or dinners with colleagues. They were the (only) parts of the home that were always kept squeaky clean and presentable to the outside world. How times have changed. In many countries, the new must-have architectural addition is the so-called great room. Great rooms integrate kitchen, living, and dining areas into one wall-less or semiwalled space. Flooring variations, steps, food preparation islands, or other forms of counter space are used to differentiate among living/dining/kitchen areas. Unfortunately, for most of us working stiffs living in our 20- to 30-year-old houses or apartments, our great room experience will have to wait.

In our model home, the living/dining area includes all the basic entertainment devices: a stereo, large TV, video game console, and a DVD player. An aquarium has been included as a proxy for the climate impact of keeping nonhuman companions around the house. Notice that the 10-gallon (gal) tropical fish aquarium uses more electricity than the TV. That is because it runs 24 hours a day, seven days a week. Tropical fish do not survive long in cold water. Not included is the cost of electricity to run the little 40 watt light that helps us keep track of the adventures of our scaly family members. I am certainly not going to suggest that you evict your fish to save the climate. However, if you are thinking about adding fish to your family, plenty of species do perfectly well at room temperature.

Lighting often has the biggest energy impact in living/dining areas. Visitors expect the public parts of your home to be well lit. Varying lighting characteristics can improve your use of space and help to differentiate functional room elements. Establishing different lighting zones can also help the atmosphere. Of course, the first and foremost change you should make is to change to CFLs or other low-energy bulbs.

Table 4.4 Living/Dining Zone

Item/Service	Current—Where You Are			Future—Where You Want to Be			
	kWh/yr	CO_2/yr (lb)	CO_2 (kg)	kWh/yr	CO_2/yr (lb)	CO_2/yr (kg)	CO_2 Cut
Living/Dining Zone							
Aquarium	569.4	776.1	352.0	569.4	776.1	352.0	0%
Clock	17.5	23.9	10.8	17.5	23.9	10.8	0%
DVD	2.0	2.7	1.2	2.0	2.7	1.2	0%
Stereo (large)	210.6	287.0	130.2	210.6	287.0	130.2	0%
Flat screen 37 in	168.5	229.6	104.2	168.5	229.6	104.2	0%
Video game console	14.0	19.1	8.7	14.0	19.1	8.7	0%
Electric air cleaner	35.1	47.8	21.7	35.1	47.8	21.7	0%
Cable box	28.1	38.3	17.4	28.1	38.3	17.4	0%
Items Subtotal	**1,045.2**	**1,424.6**	**646.2**	**1,045.2**	**1,424.6**	**646.2**	**0%**
Lighting Sheet							
Incandescent Watts (W)							
40 W (4)	224.6	306.2	138.9	56.2	76.55	34.7	**75%**
75 W (1)	105.3	143.5	65.1	28.1	38.27	17.4	**73%**
100 W (10)	1,404.0	1,913.7	868.0	407.2	554.96	2,51.7	**71%**
Lighting Subtotal	**1,733.9**	**2,363.4**	**1,072.0**	**491.4**	**669.8**	**303.8**	**72%**
Total Living/Dining	**2,779.2**	**3,788.0**	**1,718.2**	**1,536.6**	**2,094.4**	**950.0**	**45%**
Quick Cost Comparison							
$ Old Cost		295.98		$/kWh	0.1065		
$ New Cost		163.65					
$ Savings		132.33					

However, you might want to look at other ways of keeping your living space well lit and energy efficient. One of the reasons CFL lighting is not popular in some countries is because some consumers are turned off by the slightly lower lumen output and/or differing color characteristics. Installing recessed lighting with reflective elements can help to alleviate these problems. For point display lighting, such as halogen tract lighting used to illuminate small areas, light-emitting diode (LED) bulbs are becoming increasingly popular. The life span of LED bulbs is about 100,000 hours, or more than 10 times longer than their CFL counterpart. Energy use is also comparable or even superior. LED bulbs are effective point sources of light, which make them appropriate replacements for some halogen track lighting applications.

LED bulbs are effective point sources of light.

There is another wonderful source of home illumination— sunlight. Because of their relatively large size, living/dining areas often offer plenty of potential for passive solar elements, such as larger windows and skylights that make direct use of the sun's energy without solar panels or some other device. While the subject of passive solar design is too big to broach here, you might want to explore simple ways you can maximize the use of sunlight throughout your house.

Explore simple ways you can maximize the use of sunlight throughout your house.

Here is just one quick design suggestion: Install solar tube lighting. Solar tubes are basically mini round skylights. Because they are essentially wide-open pipes, they are compact and much easier and less expensive to install than skylights. They often include reflective recessed lighting, which can be used at night. Tubes can also be sealed at night to reduce heat loss. On the down side, they are typically no more than 12 inches (3.5 cm) in diameter, reducing the amount of light they can bring into your home.

If you make the suggested changes to your living/dining zone you can reduce your carbon dioxide output by 45% (1,693 lb/768 kg), save $132 in energy costs, and win yourself a Bronze Medal.

The Kitchen

Now, let's move over to the kitchen. Have you ever counted all the appliances you use to prepare and cook your daily meals? Many of us squirrel away popcorn poppers, bread makers, blenders, and electric cutting knives in nooks, cabinets, and drawers so we are not even aware of all of the must-have goodies that inhabit our cooking domain until we need them.

The list of energy-using kitchen items in Table 4.5 is far from exhaustive. Most kitchens have even more stuff. Take a look at typical energy-use values. Many of them are through the roof. Manufacturers of certain large items, such as refrigerators, freezers, and dishwashers

Table 4.5 **Kitchen Zone**

Item/Service	Current—Where You Are			Future—Where You Want to Be			
	kWh/yr	CO_2/yr (lb)	CO_2 (kg)	kWh/yr	CO_2/yr (lb)	CO_2/yr (kg)	CO_2 Cut
Kitchen zone							
Air corn popper	5.8	7.9	3.6	5.8	7.9	3.6	0%
Blender	2.1	2.9	1.3	2.1	2.9	1.3	0%
Bread maker	70.7	96.4	43.7	70.7	96.4	43.7	0%
Coffeemaker	105.3	143.5	65.1	105.3	143.5	65.1	0%
Can opener	0.7	1.0	0.4	0.0	0.0	0.0	100%
Food processor	47.7	65.1	29.5	47.7	65.1	29.5	0%
Garbage disposal	7.9	10.8	4.9	7.9	10.8	4.9	0%
Juicer	31.6	43.1	19.5	0.0	0.0	0.0	100%
Microwave	87.8	119.6	54.3	87.8	119.6	54.3	0%
Rice cooker	114.1	155.5	70.5	114.1	155.5	70.5	0%
Slow cooker	62.4	85.1	38.6	62.4	85.1	38.6	0%
Toaster	38.6	52.6	23.9	38.6	52.6	23.9	0%
Refrigerator 23 cu ft	665.8	907.4	411.6	665.8	907.4	411.6	0%
Dishwasher	252.7	344.5	156.2	0.0	0.0	0.0	100%
Range stove top	877.5	1,196.0	542.5	877.5	1,196.0	542.5	0%
Range oven	912.6	1,243.9	564.2	912.6	1,243.9	564.2	0%
Items Subtotal	**3,283.3**	**4,475.1**	**2,029.9**	**2,998.3**	**4,086.7**	**1,853.7**	**9%**
Lighting Sheet							
Incandescent Watts (W)							
40 W (4)	224.6	306.2	138.9	56.2	76.5	34.7	75%
100 W (8)	1,123.2	1,530.9	694.4	325.7	444.0	201.4	71%
Lighting Subtotal	**1,347.8**	**1,837.1**	**833.3**	**381.9**	**520.5**	**236.1**	**72%**
Total Kitchen	**4,631.1**	**6,312.2**	**2,863.2**	**3,380.2**	**4,607.2**	**2,089.8**	**27%**
Quick Cost Comparison							
$ Old Cost		493.22		$/kWh	0.107		
$ New Cost		359.99					
$ Savings		**133.23**					

participate in the Energy Star program, but most products do not have energy-efficient equivalents. Why? Consumers don't seem to care. Over the past few years, I have quizzed sales associates in Japan, the United States, and Canada about the energy use of small kitchen appliances. Few know how to respond. Most have never been asked.

Let's first discuss stove-top cooking. One of the main keys to heating and cooling anything is to ensure that as much energy as possible is used for its intended purpose. This reveals a serious downside to stove-top cooking. If you heat a pot of water on an electric stove top, most of the electrical energy, as with the incandescent lightbulb, goes straight into the air. Natural gas is slightly more efficient because the flame surrounds the surface of the cooking receptacle, but lots of heat is still lost. Also, kettle/pan design is very important. How well does the pan conduct and distribute heat? What percent of the kettle/pan directly contacts the heat source? Is it well insulated so that heated or cooled water will stay at a desired temperature for any length of time? Most thin stainless steel, aluminum, or glass pots and pans or kettles fail in all of these areas.

> One of the main keys to heating anything is to ensure that as much energy as possible is used for its intended purpose.

When choosing the proper stove-top cooking appliances, consider the fuel used to keep your stove top hot. Natural gas combustion produces about one-third fewer GHG emissions than coal, the electricity generation fuel of choice in most countries. Also with gas, unlike electricity, little energy is lost in production and transmission to your home. So in most regions, natural gas is the most environmentally friendly choice.

Enclosed and insulated cooking devices with integrated heating elements are usually more energy efficient. In our family, rice and tea are two staples. Rice cookers use lots of energy, about 650 watts, but cooking five cups of steamed rice in a pan on an electric stove top uses more than twice as much energy. Sealed kettles are wonderful tools for heating water. We use a Japanese-style two-liter water kettle for all water heating. It has an internal heating element, is fully insulated, and has a dual temperature control that keeps water warm after initial boiling. During its short boiling cycle, it uses almost 900 watts (a small electric stove-top burner uses 1,200 watts, and a large one uses 2,500 watts), but it will keep water warm for many hours. An added benefit is that boiling water also removes chlorine and bacteria, lessening the (perceived) need for bottled H_2O. Also, when you clean your own water, you know

> When you clean your own water, you know what you are getting.

what you are getting. "Counterfeit" bottled water is a common problem in many countries. For instance, an analysis of bottled water in Beijing found that about one-half of all bottles sold contained unprocessed tap water.

Another much maligned but relatively efficient heating device is the microwave oven. Microwaves are almost always more efficient than gas or electric ovens. One problem with conventional ovens is that they have much larger cooking cavities, usually larger than necessary for whatever you are cooking. The bigger the space, the more energy it takes to heat. Also, oven cooking is much slower so a significant amount of heat is lost during the longer cooking process. Of course, microwaving can negatively affect the taste and consistency of many foods. For ovenlike results, try a smaller countertop convection oven (Goodall, 2007). Convection ovens have a fan than evenly distributes heated air throughout the cooking cavity. This results in faster cooking times and more evenly cooked food. Be sure to purchase an oven that is well insulated. The better the insulation, the less the heat dissipates through the wall of the cooker (which also reduces fire risk or accidental burning of the operator).

Do we really need all of our electronic kitchen gadgets when two hands and a knife will do the job just as well? Most of us can probably live without juicers and electric can openers (or pick you own poison). One final item I strongly suggest you consider not using is your dishwasher. For centuries, we have gotten along perfectly well without them. Most dishwashers already require us to rinse cups, forks, and spoons prior to use. Some dishwashers clean with water force and high temperatures that are sometimes so high they can etch glassware. The typical dishwasher spews more than 344 lb (156 kg) of carbon dioxide into the air every year.

Of course, sink washing also uses water. So in order to really save energy and H_2O it is important to control how much water you use. Most faucets spray out 2.5 to 3 gal per minute (gpm) of water. Consider installing a 1.5 gpm (5.5 liter/minute[L/m]) swivel aerator (the nozzle at the end of the faucet) with an adjustable flow lever. Or, to really control how much water you use, try filling up a container with warm soapy water on the left side of the sink and another container with cold water on the right side for rinsing.

Making these small changes in conjunction with moving to all-CFL lighting reduces our kitchen zone carbon dioxide emissions by 27% (well into the Bronze Medal range) and electricity costs by $133.

I strongly suggest you consider not using your dishwasher.

The Bathroom

Another living space that has received a real makeover in recent years is the bathroom. No longer just places where humans go to do their "business," bathrooms have become showcases for luxury and relaxation. Old ceramic tiles have been replaced by Italian marble. Granite countertops and matching his-and-her sinks abound. Why have only one shower when you can have two? It is also increasingly frequent for these massive bathrooms to open up into equally large walk-in closets, many of which would qualify as separate bedrooms in older-generation abodes.

Well, I am afraid that our model household has not quite reached that level of bathing and grooming extravagance. However, there is plenty of space in the downloadable Comprehensive Diet Plan worksheet (www.climatediet.com/tables.asp) for you to add your own items: massive whirlpool hot tubs, heated flooring, prodigious vanity lighting, and on and on, if you want to keep track of the energy use of these accoutrements.

The bathrooms worksheet analyzes the energy-use characteristics of two identical bathrooms. Most of the electrical gadgets we use to groom and maintain ourselves use relatively little electricity, with one major exception—the infamous hair dryer. A typical hair dryer generates around 140 to 150 lb of carbon dioxide a year. I know that I am taking a bit of a risk by suggesting this, but could you consider forgoing this small wonder of modern technology? Unless you live in a very wet climate, hair dries by itself in just a few minutes.

> A typical hair dryer generates around 140 to 150 lb of carbon dioxide a year.

Like kitchens, bathrooms can really suck up the dollars if you do not rein in warm-water use. Saving water is always important, especially in drought-prone or arid regions (which are growing by the day). However, whenever you heat water with fossil fuels, there are climate consequences. Showers and sink faucets are the biggest energy hogs. The typical shower uses up to 3 gpm of warm or hot water (12 L/m is typical in the United Kingdom). Sink faucets typically use 2.5 gpm (9.5 L/m). This is a totally unnecessary extravagance. For a few dollars you can purchase a 1.5 gpm showerhead (5 L/m is common in the United Kingdom) and experience equally good results. For sink faucets where the main activity is hand washing, consider installing a 0.5 gpm aerator (1.7 L/m) for even more energy and water savings.

> Showers and sink faucets are the biggest energy hogs.

Table 4.6 Bathrooms Zone

Item/Service	Current—Where You Are			Future—Where You Want to Be			
	kWh/yr	CO₂/yr (lb)	CO₂ (kg)	kWh/yr	CO₂/yr (lb)	CO₂/yr (kg)	CO₂ Cut
Bathrooms Zone							
Bath 1							
Curling iron	5.4	7.3	3.3	5.4	7.3	3.3	0%
Electric toothbrush	0.0	0.0	0.0	0.0	0.0	0.0	0%
Hair dryer	105.3	143.5	65.1	0.0	0.0	0.0	100%
Electric shaver	0.0	0.0	0.0	0.0	0.0	0.0	0%
Vent fan	42.1	57.4	26.0	42.1	57.4	26.0	0%
Electric air cleaner	35.1	47.8	21.7	35.1	47.8	21.7	0%
Item Subtotal	**187.9**	**256.2**	**116.2**	**82.6**	**112.6**	**51.1**	**56%**
Bathroom 2							
Curling iron	5.4	7.3	3.3	5.4	7.3	3.3	0%
Electric toothbrush	0.0	0.0	0.0	0.0	0.0	0.0	0%
Hair dryer	105.3	143.5	65.1	0.0	0.0	0.0	100%
Vent fan	42.1	57.4	26.0	42.1	57.4	26.0	0%
Item Subtotal	**152.8**	**208.3**	**94.5**	**47.5**	**64.7**	**29.4**	**69%**
Lighting Sheet							
Incandescent Watts (W)							
40 W (6)	168.5	229.6	104.2	42.1	57.4	26.0	75%
100 W (4)	280.8	382.7	173.7	81.4	111.0	50.3	71%
Lighting Subtotal	**449.3**	**612.4**	**278.0**	**123.6**	**168.4**	**76.4**	**73%**
Total Bathrooms	**790.0**	**1,076.8**	**488.6**	**253.7**	**345.8**	**156.8**	**68%**
Quick Cost Comparison							
$ Old Cost		84.14		**$/kWh**	0.1065		
$ New Cost		27.02					
$ Savings		57.12					

Toilets do not use hot water, but they can really falter when it comes to water waste. The typical flush uses 3–4 gal (11.5–15 L). For an investment of a few hundred dollars, you can purchase a dual-flush toilet that will reduce this number by two-thirds. In the United States, the gold standard is a 1.6 to 0.7 gal toilet, while in the European Union 4 L/2 L (1.1/0.5 gal) toilets are widely available. If you want to save money but like the toilet you have, you can cut water use by simply filling up a jug, such as a plastic water bottle, with water and placing it in your toilet water tank. Your tank will fill up faster, as part of the space used for new water is displaced by the jug.

Our demand on natural water supplies is immense. In the United States, average per capita use clocks in at more than 107.5 gal (406.9 L) per person per day, or more than 39,000 gal (147,615 L) per person per year (EPA, 2007). It is also important to note that even unheated water delivery generates GHG emissions. Finding, storing, distributing, and recycling water affects land use and requires energy. The climate impact of water use varies widely depending on spatial, climatic, technological, and geological factors. However, it is still useful to look at an example. One Australian study estimates that 528 lb (240 kg) of carbon dioxide equivalent are generated per 26,420 gal (100,000 L) of water provided to consumers. The annual estimated embodied emissions for maintaining a water system generates an additional 286 pounds (130 kg) per year. This adds up to a whopping 814 pounds (370 kg) of carbon dioxide equivalent emissions per 26,420 gal (100,000 L) of water used, or more than 3,300 pounds (1,500 kg) of emissions for an American family of four. Thankfully, Australian residential water use is about half that of U.S. residents (Carbonneutral, 2006).

If you can follow the few suggestions detailed above, plus swap your incandescent vanity lighting for CFLs or equivalent bulbs, you can reduce your nonwater-related electricity use by 68%, cut your energy bill by $57, and earn a Silver Medal.

The Laundry/Utility Room

Our bathroom example dovetails nicely into our next topic, washing/drying and water heating. We already noted the high cost of heating liquid in the kitchen. That number pales in comparison to the tens of thousands of gallons of heated water that pass through our household water heater every year. In our model house, water heating is the second highest contributor to global warming. A typical 50 gal (190 L) central water heater in high heat mode spews out around 6,500 lb (2,951 kg) of carbon dioxide per year.

Like the hair dryer and standard electric coil stove top, mass market water heaters have not changed much in recent years. However, making small adjustments to how we use this dated technology and the water that it heats can have a major impact on the atmosphere. The easiest first step we can take is to simply turn down the temperature. Energy Star energy-use estimates are based on water heaters running at full bore (140° F or 60° C) 7 days a week, 365 days a year. This is neither necessary nor desirable, even if you do not care about the environmental impact (an amazing number of people still set their water heater thermostat this high). Few people can stand water this hot. Extremely hot water can damage some fabrics. Also, water at 140° F (60° C) does not provide many additional antibacterial or other antiseptic benefits. When we wash our hands, dishes, or clothes we almost always use some type of soap or detergent that kills most little nasties. The best way to kill bacteria is to hang your clothes in the sun for a few hours. This strategy saves energy on the washing and drying side of the cleanliness equation. Plenty of detergents on the market are designed for cold-water washing. Why not try one (preferably a biodegradable brand) and see how it works? Adjust your hot water heater temperature to 104° F (40° C) or less. That should supply more than enough warm water to get you through the day.

Another sad fact about water heaters is that much of the heat from the water dissipates (referred to as *standby loss*) before we even get a chance to use it. Most of us use hot water in spurts, especially in the morning, followed by long periods of nonuse. During these periods, heat floats into thin air. Water tank walls are notoriously underinsulated. Water pipes also have poor insulating qualities. One way to get around this problem is to invest in a tankless water heater. These devices, common in Asia and parts of Europe, only heat water when you need it. Unfortunately, tankless heaters are much more expensive than their conventional equivalents. An alternative and less costly strategy is to wrap your heater and exposed pipes in precut insulation wrap (Consumer Research Council, 2005).

Adjust your hot water heater temperature to 104° F (40° C) or less.

Table 4.7 Laundry/Utility Zone

Item/service	Current—Where You Are			Future—Where You Want to Be			
	kWh/yr	CO_2/yr (lbs)	CO_2 (kg)	kWh/yr	CO_2/yr (lbs)	CO_2/yr (kg)	CO_2 Cut
Wash/Utility Zone							
Washing machine	529.2	721.3	327.2	235.2	320.6	145.4	56%
Clothes dryer	885.9	1207.5	547.7	885.9	1,207.5	547.7	0%
Hot water (50 gal)	4,818.0	6,566.9	2,978.7	3,212.0	4,378.0	1,985.8	33%
Vacuum (hand)	3.2	4.3	2.0	3.2	4.3	2.0	0%
Vacuum (upright)	27.4	37.3	16.9	27.4	37.3	16.9	0%
Iron	50.5	68.9	31.2	37.9	51.7	23.4	25%
Electric air cleaner	35.1	47.8	21.7	35.1	47.8	21.7	0%
Items subtotal	6,349.3	8,654.1	3,925.4	4,436.7	6,047.2	2,743.0	30%
Lighting sheet							
Incandescent Watts (W)							
100 W (2)	280.8	382.7	173.60	81.4	111.0	50.3	71%
Lighting sheet	280.8	382.7	182.12	81.4	111.0	52.8	71%
Total Laundry/Utility	6,630.1	9,036.8	4,107.5	4,518.1	6,158.2	2,795.8	32%
Quick Cost Comparison							
$ Old Cost		706.11		$/kWh	0.1065		
$ New Cost		481.18					
$ Savings		224.93					

Note: A 33% reduction (from 60° C) in hot water heater temperature is included in the calculations.

Of course, we can also reduce water heating costs by simply using less water. Buying a smaller water tank may condition your family to understanding the value of heated water and should also cut down on energy waste during times of nonuse. Most Europeans get by with much smaller water tanks than North Americans. Try taking five-minute showers rather than tub baths. Wait until it is full to run your washing machine. Also, install low-flow faucets/shower heads throughout your home.

Table 4.7 provides some possible suggestions for cutting back in other areas of the laundry/utility zone. In keeping with the overall conserving spirit of this book, I only recommend one new purchase for our model house: a new washing machine. Front-loading machines are so much more efficient in energy and water use that they are hard to pass up. The typical Energy Star model uses only 0.6 kWh versus 1.35 kWh per load for a top-loading model (or more if your machine is more than five years old). Most localities have rebate programs for more efficient models. For drying, think about using the sun during warmer months (600 plus lb of savings or 272 kg). Or try hanging clothes indoors during periods of inclement weather, preferably near a heater/AC vent or other conditioned area of your home. You can reduce emissions from ironing by 25% simply by using the low setting or by making future clothing purchases that require less ironing. Finally, don't forget to change your lightbulbs.

If you make the suggested changes to our model home, you can cut your carbon dioxide emissions by 32%, reduce energy costs by $225, and win a Bronze Medal to boot.

Tips Summary

Model home changes to interior zones:

- ✓ Switch incandescent lighting to CFL equivalent in all zones.
- ✓ Install one new ceiling fan (bedroom 1).
- ✓ Replace space heater with an electric blanket (bedroom 2).
- ✓ Purchase a new Energy Star 19-inch LCD monitor (bedroom 3).
- ✓ Purchase a new Energy Star printer (bedroom 3).
- ✓ Cease using home copier (bedroom 3).
- ✓ Install solar tube lighting fixtures (living/dining).
- ✓ Cease using two small appliances (kitchen).
- ✓ Cease using dishwasher (kitchen).
- ✓ Cease using hair dryers (bathrooms).

✓ Purchase a front-loading washing machine (laundry/utility).

✓ Reduce bathroom water use by taking shorter showers (laundry/utility).

✓ Wrap water heaters and leading piping in insulation to minimize heat loss (laundry/utility).

✓ Reduce hot water heater setting from 140° F (60° C) to 104° F (40° C; laundry/utility).

✓ Consider forgoing use of hot water for washing clothes (laundry/utility).

✓ Air dry washed clothes whenever possible (laundry/utility).

For even more savings:

✓ Try living in a smaller home.

✓ Use room fans to more evenly distribute conditioned air.

✓ Cut back on watching TV, which saves time and energy for more important things in life.

✓ Always purchase high-efficiency office equipment if needed.

✓ Be aware of the potential climate impact of nonhuman companions.

✓ Design living/dining room areas to maximize sunlight.

✓ Create living/dining room lighting zones that allow you to maintain high illumination in actively used areas while reducing illumination in unused areas.

✓ Consider installing natural gas piping in kitchen/utility areas to allow use of natural gas appliances.

✓ Use high-efficiency cooking pots/kettles to maximize heat transfer and minimize heat loss during cooking.

✓ Rid your life of unnecessary small appliances.

✓ Install water-efficient aerators on all kitchen and bathroom faucets and low-flow showerheads.

✓ Consider installing dual-flush, low water-use toilets.

Reduce bathroom water use by taking shorter showers.

Rid your life of unnecessary small appliances.

Finding the Right Balance: Heating, Cooling, and Outside Spaces

5

Heating and Cooling Basics

When it comes to household GHG emissions, heating and cooling are near the top of the list. Depending on where you live, heating and cooling generate between 30% and 60% of total nontransport emissions. Conditioning air is a complex business. Numerous factors, including building size, design and materials, age, external climatic factors, and personal comfort preferences, affect how we control air temperature. To simplify matters, this discussion is broken down into three sections:

✓   Finding the right temperature (no cost).

✓   Keeping conditioned air where you want it (low cost).

✓   Purchasing energy-efficient systems (higher initial cost but bigger long-term benefits).

Our model house was initially fitted with a 78% efficient natural gas, air-blown furnace that meets 2006 minimum U.S./Canadian efficiency standards. This efficiency level exceeds most of the current average installed capacity, which ranges from 60% to 70% depending on which country you live in (Goodall, 2007). Our model home was built decades ago, so walls, windows, insulation, and other forms of weatherproofing are subpar by new-home standards.

Finding the Right Temperature

Finding the right temperature is a very subjective process. For most Americans, 72° F (22° C) is the norm. However, you would be hard pressed to find many Japanese families who set their thermostats (most do not even have central heating) this high in the winter. Since the late 1970s the U.S. government has recommended that all citizens maintain their winter indoor temperature at 68° F (20° C) and even lower when they are not at home. However, few have heeded this call for conservation. What difference do a few degrees make? For our model house, reducing the daytime and evening temperature from 72° F to 70° F (22° C to 21° C) and overnight temperatures from 68° F to 66° F (20° C to 19° C) will reduce yearly carbon dioxide emissions by close to 10% a year. Reducing temperatures an additional 2° F (1.6° C) will accrue an additional 10%

in savings (Pacific Gas and Electric, 2007). For an investment of less than $100, you can purchase a programmable thermostat that will automatically change the temperature for you, which will reduce your emissions an additional 16%. Sounds like a good deal to me. If you still feel cold, try throwing on a sweater. Finally, you may want to consider whether the whole house needs to be heated or if heating only one or two rooms is sufficient. This may not yet be an option in Ottawa or Helsinki, but it might be more doable if you live where it rarely freezes during the winter.

Keeping Conditioned Air Where You Want It

Most energy savings books and manuals state that the best way to cut your energy use is to run out and buy new technology. Sure, there are plenty of superefficient heaters and coolers on the market that do accrue substantial energy performance gains over older products. But before you think about buying one of these newfangled contraptions, first make sure that your living space efficiently retains newly conditioned air where you want it, inside your house or apartment. If you have a poorly sealed, drafty building, even the best heating system is not going to keep you warm.

If you have a poorly sealed, drafty building, even the best heating system is not going to keep you warm.

While we might not notice it, oxygen, carbon dioxide, nitrogen, and a host of other gases and vapors constantly flow through our structures. Air flow is necessary to allow the transfer of clean air while permitting harmful gases to exit. Having an efficient system of air control and exchange is critical to creating a safer and more climate-friendly house. This system includes basement walls and floors, above-grade walls, roof, doors, and windows.

As a general rule, heat moves wherever there is a difference in temperature, from warmer areas to colder ones. Heat can go in any direction; up, down, or sideways. So highly permeable parts of the building envelope, that is, poorly insulated walls, windows, ceilings, floors, or foundations can lead to significant energy loss. Air in/air out is primarily a problem of infiltration, the actual flow of air into and outside the envelope. Poor insulation results in conduction or radiation losses through elements of the envelope. Changes in air pressure caused by wind, interior temperature variations, or combustion and ventilation can force air out. High humidity can cause condensation and frost buildup on windows, which also causes heat loss.

So the key to having a warmer structure is to do whatever you can to seal your building envelope so that it holds conditioned air in and keeps excessive amounts of unconditioned air out. The best way to do this is to increase the thermal insulating, or R-value, of your walls, ceilings, windows, and floors. *R-value* refers to the insulating properties of building materials, namely, their conductive, radiation, and thermal resistance. Higher is better. Older houses, like our model home, often lack adequate insulation. When we moved into our forty-year-old Mercer Island house, it had no wall insulation whatsoever, and the basement was so cold it could barely be used in winter. It also has large bay windows that have even lower R-values than noninsulated walls. An absence of door sweeps and poorly sealed window and door cavities added to the problem.

We invited a contractor certified in Leadership in Energy and Environmental Design (LEED) to the house to assess the situation. He suggested thousands of dollars in new windows and door additions. There are plenty of high R-value window products on the market, ranging from double-paned tinted designs to triple-paned insulating low-E (emittance)/argon gas-filled windows. We ended up opting for a much more affordable solution. For about $1,300, we doubled the thickness of our attic insulation, installed door sweeps, applied caulk around every window, and sealed all door openings with tubular and closed cell foam weather stripping. Our heating bill dropped by 15%.

Beyond doors and windows, there are plenty of other possible paths for warm air to find its way out of your building. Here is a short list of other typical problem areas:

- ✓ Under sinks and bathtubs (porcelain has very poor insulating characteristics).
- ✓ Around piping and ductwork.
- ✓ Wall or foundation cracks.
- ✓ Fireplace dampers and walls (fireplaces are one of the worst offenders when it comes to sucking air out of your structure).
- ✓ Around light fixtures, exhaust fans, and electrical outlets.
- ✓ Holes for wiring or plumbing.
- ✓ Doors or hatches to unheated areas like attics.

✓   Around garage doors (consider insulated doors that fit snuggly with the floor surface and other parts of the door-opening cavity).

How much insulation or weather stripping is enough? It really depends on where you live. For instance, in higher latitudes (for example, Yukon or Labrador) Natural Resources Canada (2004) recommends R-values of 30, 17, 51, and 51 for walls, basement walls, roofs, and floors, respectively. For Toronto and central Canada (or the equivalent), NRC recommends R-values of 23, 17, 38, and 38. In Vancouver and similar areas, it recommends R-values of 17, 17, 26, and 27. And yes, too much of a good thing can also hurt you. Overly "tight" envelopes can restrict air flow, causing buildup of toxic gases including radon and carbon monoxide. To counteract this, tightly sealed homes should have an active air-to-air heat exchanger (fans that periodically remove air from the interior of the building) that encourages internal-external air flow (NRC, 2004).

Overly "tight" envelopes can restrict air flow, causing buildup of toxic gases.

The U.S. EPA R-values for walls, basement walls, roofs, and floors include:

✓   Southeast: walls R-13 to R-25; basement walls R-11 to R-19; roof R-38 to R-49; floor R-13 to R-19.

✓   Midwest/New England: walls R-11 to R-28; basement walls R-13 to R-19; roof R-38 to R-49; floor R-25.

✓   West Coast, Mid-Atlantic: walls R-11 to R-22; basement walls R-11 to R-19; roof R-38 to R-49; floor R-13 to R-25

(Energy Star, 2007b)

Table 5.1 International City Climate Comparisons

North American Cities	International City with Equivalent Climate
Anchorage	St. Petersburg
Atlanta	Rome
Chicago	Berlin
Honolulu	Carnes, Australia
Los Angeles	Sydney, Australia
New York City	Amsterdam
Ottawa	Beijing
Vancouver	Tokyo

Table 5.1 provides international city comparisons you can use to roughly determine the level of insulation recommended for your latitude and climate.

Purchasing Energy-Efficient Systems

Table 5.2 illustrates the effect of making the transition from a 78% efficient gas furnace to an Energy Star–rated 90% efficient one. An oil furnace example is also included. Our model home is in the New England zone. Therefore, installing a more efficient furnace will reduce carbon dioxide emissions by around 27%. Most people will save even more because average installed historical efficiency ratings are under 70% in most OECD countries. According to the U.S. Department of Energy, a typical Energy Star gas furnace costs about $4,000 versus $2,700 for a 78% efficient model. This is an investment that many of us may not be able to immediately make. However, the climate benefits are clear.

> Installing a more efficient furnace will reduce carbon dioxide emissions by around 27%.

Far more efficient heaters (up to 98%) are also available. Other more expensive technologies, such as air and geothermal heat pumps, offer additional emissions reductions. For even more savings, make sure all heating ducts are well sealed, and have your furnace/boiler regularly serviced. Finally, the table reveals that natural gas produces fewer emissions than heating oil to heat an equivalent home so if you are thinking about replacing your old oil boiler, seriously consider natural gas.

> Make sure all heating ducts are well sealed, and have your furnace/boiler regularly serviced.

Air-Conditioning

For people living closer to the Equator, air-conditioning is a central concern. For cool air, the same rules apply. First, you need to decide how cool is cool enough. Increasing daytime cooling temperatures from 72° F to 76° F (22° C to 24° C) will substantially cut your emissions. Properly sealing your house keeps cool air in and warm air out. Also, is central air-conditioning really necessary or is cooling one or two rooms sufficient? If the latter is the case, installing one or two room air conditioners is probably a more climate-friendly choice.

Table 5.2 Heating Zone Options

| | Future—Where You Want to Be | | | | Current—Where You Are | | | | | |
| | Energy Star AFUE[a] 90% | | | | Conventional AFUE 78% | | | | | |
Furnace (gas) 85,000 Btu/hr	Therm/ year	$ Cost year	CO₂/yr (lb)	CO₂/yr (kg)	Therm/ year	$ Cost year	CO₂/yr (lb)	CO₂/yr (kg)	CO₂ diff.[b] (lb)	CO₂ diff. (kg)
Region (U.S.)										
Pacific	511.0	643.9	5,968.5	2,707.3	703.0	885.8	8,211.0	3,724.5	(2,242.6)	(1,017.21)
New England	768.0	967.7	8,970.2	4,068.8	1,055.0	1,329.3	12,322.4	5,589.3	(3,352.2)	(1,520.51)
SE Atlantic	643.0	810.2	7,510.2	3,406.6	883.0	1,112.6	10,313.4	4,678.1	(2,803.2)	(1,271.51)
Mid Atlantic	710.0	894.6	8,292.8	3,761.6	976.0	1,229.8	11,399.7	5,170.8	(3,106.9)	(1,409.26)

| | Energy Star AFUE 86% | | | | Conventional AFUE 80% | | | | | |
Furnace (oil) 85,000 Btu/hr	Gallons/ year	$ Cost year	CO₂/yr (lb)	CO₂/yr (kg)	Gallons/ year	$ Cost year	CO₂/yr (lb)	CO₂/yr (kg)	CO₂ diff. (lb)	CO₂ diff. (kg)
Region (U.S.)										
Pacific	366.0	746.6	8,190.7	3,715.2	493.0	1,005.7	11,032.8	5,004.4	(2,842.1)	(1,289.17)
New England	552.0	1,126.1	12,353.2	5,603.3	740.0	1,509.6	16,560.5	7,511.7	(4,207.3)	(1,908.38)
SE Atlantic	462.0	942.5	10,339.1	4,689.7	619.0	1,262.8	13,852.6	6,283.4	(3,513.5)	(1,593.70)
Mid Atlantic	511.0	1,042.4	11,435.7	5,187.1	684.0	1,395.4	15,307.2	6,943.2	(3,871.6)	(1,756.11)

Note: New England gas value used for diet. Weatherproofing adjustment: If minor weatherproofing, subtract 10% from new carbon value. If major weatherproofing, subtract 20% from new carbon value. For each 1°C room temperature change, subtract 10% from old carbon value. If programmable thermostat, subtract 16%. In this case the Energy Star product comes with programmable thermostat as standard. Separate 10% reductions were made for minor weatherproofing and 2°C reduction in average interior temperature are not included in the table calculations but are included in chapter 9, Table 9.1, and Table 9.2 and in the Tips Summary at the end of this chapter.

1 gallon heating oil = 1.39 therms, 1 therm natural gas = 11.68 lb CO₂. Assumes $1.26 per therm, $2.04 per gallon, 16.1 lb CO₂ emissions per therm of heating oil and 2,000 sq ft home area. (gallons oil x 1.39) x (16.1) = Total heating oil CO₂ emissions.

[a] Annual Fuel Utilization Efficiency

[b] difference

Visit www.climatediet.com/tables.asp to compute your own values.

Source: Energy Star (2007). Lifecycle Worksheets: Heating.

Two ratios are commonly used to measure air conditioner efficiency. The energy-efficient ratio (EER) measures how much cooling effect is generated by each unit of electricity. The seasonal energy efficiency ratio (SEER) measures the cooling efficiency of an air conditioner over an entire cooling season. In both cases, higher is better. In the United States and Canada, Energy Star–rated air conditioners are at least 10% more efficient than those that meet minimum standards.

Our model house is located in a climate equivalent to that of Boston. It assumes the use of two 10,000 Btu room air conditioners. Total carbon dioxide emissions per season for two conventional room air conditioners are 2,149 lb (976 kg) versus 1,857 lb (843 kg) for Energy Star–rated versions. Notice that as you travel south, as temperatures rise, carbon dioxide savings from converting to an Energy Star unit increase significantly. Table 5.3 also illustrates the comparative effect of running room air conditioners versus central units. In Boston, running three room units results in lower emissions than one central unit. Finally, like heating systems, an Energy Star rating is far from the gold standard in efficiency. Air-conditioning units with EER values of 20 or more are widely available. How much money and carbon dioxide you can save by purchasing a more efficient model largely depends on where you live and how well your house is sealed. As with heating systems, it is essential that you choose the right size unit to fit your space. Check the manufacturer literature for sizing information.

One other factor to consider is humidity. Wringing water out of the air is a service provided by air conditioners that is sometimes more crucial than cooling per se. An air conditioner does this by virtue of its evaporator core, which is necessary in relatively muggy conditions. But just relying on the air conditioner alone is often not enough. Be sure to turn your home humidifier off, keep windows shut whenever the outside dew point temperature is above 60°F (15.5°C), take shorter showers, avoid running the dishwasher, and cover all water sources like coffee cups, electric fountains, or waterfalls. If you live in a dry climate, an evaporative unit or "swamp cooler" (which draws exterior air into special pads soaked with water, where the air is cooled by evaporation) may save energy and money. However, some studies connect evaporative coolers to various health problems, so do your research before purchasing one of these systems.

> Table 5.3 also illustrates the comparative effect of running room air conditioners versus central units.

Table 5.3 Air-Conditioning Zone

City	Future—Where You Want to Go					Current—Where You Are					
	Cool hours year	kWh year	$Cost year	CO₂/yr (lb)	CO₂/yr (kg)	kWh year	$Cost year	CO₂/yr (lb)	CO₂/yr (kg)	CO₂ diff.[a] (lb)	CO₂ diff. (kg)
Room A/C	E. Star	Conv.[b]									
EER[c] (New)	10.7	9.7									
Btu/hr	10,000	10,000									
Cost/kWh	0.107	0.107									
CO₂ lb/kWh	1.36	1.36									
# units	1	1									
Atlanta	1,484	1,386.9	148	1,890.4	857.5	1,529.9	163	2,085.2	945.9	(194.9)	(88.4)
Boston	**729**	**681.3**	**73**	**928.6**	**421.2**	**751.5**	**80**	**1,024.4**	**464.6**	**(95.7)**	**(43.4)**
Chicago	683	638.3	68	870.0	394.6	704.1	75	959.7	435.3	(89.7)	(40.7)
Honolulu	5,016	4,687.9	499	6,389.5	2,898.2	5,171.1	551	7,048.3	3,197.0	(658.7)	(298.8)
Los Angeles	1,530	1,429.9	152	1,949.0	884.0	1,577.3	168	2,149.9	975.2	(200.9)	(91.1)
New York City	1,089	1,017.8	108	1,387.2	629.2	1,122.7	120	1,530.2	694.1	(143.0)	(64.9)
Seattle	282	263.6	28	359.2	162.9	290.7	31	396.3	179.7	(37.0)	(16.8)
Yours?	0	0.0	0	0.0	0.0	0.0	0	0.0	0.0	0.0	0.0
Central A/C	E. Star	Conv.									
SEER[d] (New)	12.0	10.0									
Btu/hr	36,000	36,000									

	Cost/kWh	0.107					0.107				
	CO_2 lb/kWh	1.36					1.36		1.36		
	# units	1					1		1		

City	Cool hours year	kWh year	$Cost year	CO_2/yr (lb)	CO_2/yr (kg)	kWh year	$Cost year	CO_2/yr (lb)	CO_2/yr (kg)	CO_2 (lb)	CO_2 (kg)
Atlanta	1,484	3,739.7	398	5,097.2	2,312.0	5,342.4	569	7,281.7	3,302.9	(2,184.5)	(990.9)
Boston	**729**	**1,837.1**	**196**	**2,503.9**	**1,135.8**	**2,624.4**	**279**	**3,577.1**	**1,622.5**	**(1,073.1)**	**(486.8)**

Future—Where You Want to Go | | | | | | Current—Where You Are | | | | | |

City	Cool hours year	kWh year	$Cost year	CO_2/yr (lb)	CO_2/yr (kg)	kWh year	$Cost year	CO_2/yr (lb)	CO_2/yr (kg)	CO_2 (lb)	CO_2 (kg)
Chicago	683	1,721.2	183	2,345.9	1,064.1	2,458.8	262	3,351.3	1,520.1	(1,005.4)	(456.0)
Honolulu	5,016	1,2640.3	1,346	17,228.8	7,814.8	18,058	1923	24,612.5	11,164.0	(7,383.8)	(3,349.2)
Los Angeles	1,530	3,855.6	411	5,255.2	2,383.7	5,508.0	587	7,507.4	3,405.3	(2,252.2)	(1,021.6)
New York City	1,089	2,744.3	292	3,740.5	1,696.6	3,920.4	418	5,343.5	2,423.8	(1,603.1)	(727.1)
Seattle	282	710.6	76	968.6	439.4	1,015.2	108	1,383.7	627.6	(415.1)	(188.3)
Yours?	0	0.0	0	0.0	0.0	0.0	0	0.0	0.0	0.0	0.0

Note: Electric cost kWh = 0.1066 U.S. cents 1 Btu = 0.0002929 kWh (1,000,000 Btu = 293 kWh) Assumes 2,000 sq ft home area. One lb = 0.4535924 kg. One kg = 2.204622476 lb. "Where You Want to Go" two air conditioner example includes a 10% reduction for increasing room temperature by 2°F (1.6° C). Visit www.climatediet.com/tables to compute your own values.

[a] difference

[b] conventional

[c] energy-efficient ratio

[d] seasonal energy efficiency ratio

Source: Energy Star (2007a). Estimates calculated using EPA lifecycle worksheets: Air Conditioning.

If you make the suggested changes to the heating (10% temperature reduction and 10% weatherproofing) and cooling (10% temperature increase), you can reduce your carbon footprint by around 7,500 lb (3,405 kg) and your energy costs by around $800. Sounds like a solid Bronze Medal performance for one of the more challenging areas of the home.

Managing Outside Spaces

Last but not least, let's take a quick look at the climate impact of home-based outside activities. As I mentioned before, many of us increasingly find ourselves using outside spaces, yards, decks, balconies, and so on, for activities formerly relegated to indoor areas. One case in point is dining. Patio furniture and grill manufacturers are experiencing growing demand for their products. Outdoor cooking is becoming so popular that some households are building kitchenlike permanent facilities on their patios. Unfortunately, outdoor gas and electric grills are even less efficient than their in-house brethren.

Besides your outdoor gas grill, another gas/propane accoutrement that you may want to avoid is a patio heater. It may be tempting to use one of these massive contraptions to defy the elements so you can work on your suntan on a sunny but cold spring day, but did you know that the average patio heater burns as much as 40,000 Btu of fuel per hour? That is almost half as much energy as is required to heat your entire house. With no walls or windows to stop it, all of that valuable heat goes straight up into the air along with huge amounts of carbon dioxide.

As we use our outdoor space more often, maintaining it has become an even higher priority. Table 5.4 provides a starting point for calculating the energy impact of yard maintenance. This rather minimalist list of yard tools barely touches the surface of what many people own. In the United States, most lawn mowers run on gasoline and have very inefficient engines and minimal pollution control devices, which makes them some of the most environmentally unfriendly devices around. While there is prodigious information about personal vehicle efficiency and related emissions, similar data on lawn maintenance items is scare. This is also true of gasoline-powered recreational products like jet skis, small outboard boat motors, and all terrain vehicles (ATVs). Again,

> Did you know that the average patio heater burns as much as 40,000 Btu of fuel per hour?

Table 5.4 **Yard Zone**

| Item/Service | Current—Where You Are | | | Future—Where You Want to Be | | | |
	kWh/yr	CO_2/yr (lb)	CO_2 (kg)	kWh/yr	CO_2/yr (lb)	CO_2/yr (kg)	CO_2 Cut
Yard Zone							
Electric lawn mower	45.0	61.3	27.8	22.5	30.7	13.9	50%
Chainsaw	9.2	12.5	5.7	9.2	12.5	5.7	0%
Leaf blower	11.1	15.1	6.8	0.0	0.0	0.0	100%
Circular saw	10.6	14.5	6.6	10.6	14.5	6.6	0%
Electric grill	54.0	73.6	33.4	54.0	73.6	33.4	0%
Weed trimmer	15.0	20.4	9.3	7.5	10.2	4.6	50%
Items Subtotal	144.8	197.4	89.5	103.8	141.5	64.2	28%
Lighting Sheet							
Incandescent Watts (W)							
60 W (2)	168.5	229.6	104.2	42.1	57.4	26.0	75%
100 W (4)	561.6	765.5	347.2	162.9	222.0	100.7	71%
Lighting Subtotal	730.1	995.1	451.4	205	279.4	126.7	72%
Total Yard	874.9	1,192.5	540.9	308.8	420.9	190.9	65%
Quick Cost Comparison							
$ Old Cost		93.18		$/kWh	0.1065		
$ New Cost		32.89					
$ Savings		60.29					

consumers do not seem to care much about the climate consequences of their tools and toys, so manufacturers do not care either. If you regularly use these toys you might want to include them in your Climate Diet.

Among the short list of tools on our yard worksheet, the ubiquitous lawn mower leads the pack followed by the electric weed trimmer. In the lawn care arena, electric is usually better. One suggested change: Lose the leaf blower. At 2,500 watts, it is one of the most power-hungry devices around. Raking works just as well.

In the lawn care arena, electric is usually better.

There are plenty of other outdoor items not on our list that should generally be avoided. I will mention just one—the swimming pool. If you think keeping water hot in an insulated kettle is expensive, try doing it outside where heated water is exposed to the elements. An electric pool heater can consume up to 50,000 watts. A two-horsepower pool pump uses another 2,000 watts. Operating a pool heater and pump six hours a day/90 days a year generates more than 45,000 lb (20,430 kg) of carbon dioxide, or the equivalent of operating three typical SUVs per year. If you just cannot do without your pool, try using a do-it-yourself simple solar array system to keep the water warm.

Blending In With Nature

The best way to save money and the atmosphere in your outdoor spaces is to design and use them in ways that blend in with the local environment. Think of your yard as a carbon sink (a natural repository where carbon is stored in soil, trees, and plants). Plants, trees, and even dead leaves act as carbon repositories that slow or even reverse the flow of GHGs into the air. The typical tree removes more than one ton of carbon dioxide from the atmosphere during its 40-year lifetime.

The typical tree removes more than one ton of carbon dioxide from the atmosphere during its 40-year lifetime.

Trees not only soak up carbon and supply shade, but also provide wonderful habitats for native birds, insects, and mammals. The U.S.-based National Wildlife Federation has an excellent program dedicated to educating landowners on how to transform their gardens into natural habitats for local wildlife while drastically reducing the use of pesticides, fertilizers, and water. A wildlife habitat requires the following simple elements: food and water, native plants, cover that provides some kind of shelter from weather and predators, and spaces for wildlife to mate and rear their young. Use of native plants and grasses often reduces the need for watering. Longer grass length provides added cover for small critters. Sustainable gardening practices, including the capture and reuse of natural water sources, reducing lawn areas, effective soil conservation practices, control of nonnative exotic species, and eliminating the use of all pesticides and fertilizers, all help to arrest the march of climate change (National Wildlife Federation, 2006). Almost any size space will do. Even a balcony or deck can be transformed into a living biotic environment. Also, letting nature take care of itself will save you time and money. In our model house, creating a wildlife habitat reduces the use of lawn mowers and weed trimmers by half.

Cutting back on power tool use and creating more nature-friendly outdoor space reduces yard emissions by 65% and energy costs by $60, winning you a Silver Medal.

Creating a wildlife habitat reduces the use of lawn mowers and weed trimmers by half.

Other General Recommendations for Climate-Friendly Remodeling

Beyond the dieting changes described in the last two chapters, some other general things should be considered when you begin Climate Diet modifications to your house. You really need to take a holistic approach to the project, because changes to heating, insulation, or lighting in one area inevitably affect others. One good book on this topic is Johnson and Master's (2004) *Green Remodeling: Changing the World One Room at a Time*. If you need professional help, be sure to look for a LEED-certified contractor. LEED is a building certification mostly used in commercial construction. Many large firms have decided that building more efficient offices generates energy savings, better working conditions for employees, and bragging rights to being able to call themselves green. Unfortunately, many other green ratings systems only require minimal modifications to homes (e.g., adding a few Energy Star appliances and some insulation) to get green certified. It is often difficult for consumers to tell the difference between the various shades of "greenness" provided by contractors and remodelers. Educate yourself about the difference between deep green and green washing (fake green) before agreeing to any future remodeling projects.

One more suggestion. Many consumers now use "smart meters" to keep track of real-time energy use in their homes. Placing a meter in some prominent location in your home is a wonderful way to educate yourself on how specific activities, such as baking cookies or brewing a pot of coffee, affect your electricity bill and GHG emissions.

Conclusion

I hope it is clear by now that the Climate Diet offers numerous easy-to-use strategies to cut our impact on the environment and that they can be tailored to almost any lifestyle. Most of the suggestions made in chapters 4 and 5 require little or no investment. In fact, going on a diet should save you money.

Suggested changes to our model house example reduced yearly energy costs by more than $1,600 and carbon dioxide emissions by more than 18,000 lb (8,354 kg). That is well into the Bronze range and exceeds the planned 2008–2012 Kyoto Protocol reductions. Conservation can go a very long way if we just give it a chance. I invite you to take a close look at the longer list of household items and associated climate effects in chapter 9. While this list is far from exhaustive, it should at least provide a good starting point for tailoring the Climate Diet to your own needs. Don't just limit yourself to the few changes we have discussed so far. Go for the Gold!

> Conservation can go a very long way if we just give it a chance.

Tips Summary

Model home changes to heating, cooling, and yard zones:

- ✅ Weatherize living area for 10% reduction (heating and cooling).
- ✅ Replace a 78% efficient with a 90% efficient gas furnace (heating).
- ✅ Install programmable thermostat for 16% savings.
- ✅ Reduce heat temperature by 2° F for 10% savings.
- ✅ Replace two conventional room air conditioners with Energy Star 10,000 Btu room air conditioners (cooling).
- ✅ Cease using leaf blower (yard).
- ✅ Reduce use of lawn mower and weed trimmer by 50% (yard).
- ✅ Create an easy-to-maintain, climate-appropriate wildlife habitat (yard).

For even more savings:

✓ Conduct an energy audit and carry out necessary major weatherizing activities.

✓ Reduce winter interior temperature by an additional 2° F and increase summer temperature by an additional 2° F.

✓ Properly maintain heating and cooling systems and repair ductwork when necessary.

✓ Avoid use of power yard tools, especially gas-powered ones, whenever possible. Try using a human-powered push reel mower for lawn maintenance.

✓ Avoid the use of outdoor patio heaters.

✓ Preserve natural habitats for nonhuman residents.

Shopping, Eating, Recycling, and More

6

Shopping. Few things arouse more excitement in the hearts of frenzied consumers than the allure of all things new: new cars, new shoes, new clothes. "New" is used by marketers more than any other word in the English lexicon. That "new'" car you have had your eye on looks fabulous on the showroom floor. It has a "new car" smell. Even the color is meant to convey an environmentally friendly image. It is no accident that one of the most popular hues for large SUVs is hunter green. Commercials often depict these leaf-colored vehicles traversing mountaintops or poised beside babbling brooks. Ironically, SUV owners are more likely than the average person to enjoy the great outdoors but are also disproportionately responsible for its destruction. What explains this paradox? Most consumers just do not make the connection between their buying habits and their associated effect on the environment.

How did we get so hooked on shopping? The post–World War II period heralded a golden age of industrial growth and innovation. Advances in science and technology provided a vast new array of consumer goods. These same technological advances enabled lower-cost mass production, making new products affordable to a broader swath of the population. It was not until the 1950s that must-have items, including televisions, automobiles, refrigerators, washing machines, and central heating and air-conditioning, appeared in millions of homes. Chemical industry giants offered new and better ways for convenience-hungry shoppers to make their houses cleaner, clothes cheaper, and grass greener. A growing middle class demanded bigger houses and more personal space, helping to fuel an exodus from urban cores to suburban communities in many countries. Add to this the drone of nonstop advertising; rising incomes; and, in the United States, American-style Puritanism, which dictates that material wealth is God's reward for a job well done; and frenzied overconsumption is the result.

Unfortunately, as research has borne out, there is a downside to this life of convenience and plenty. The purpose of this chapter is to help bridge the gap between actions and understanding so we can make smart consumer choices that not only satisfy our current needs, but help us to be better stewards of the climate and preserve resources for future generations.

Most consumers just do not make the connection between their buying habits and their associated effect on the environment.

The Energy Within

Though my family lives relatively modestly in comparison to most middle-class Americans, we are hardly exempt from the pressure to consume unsustainably produced products. To get a better handle on the extent to which synthetic and petroleum-based products invade our daily lives, Kela and I decided to play a little game called "Find the Oil." Oil in the house, you ask? You would be surprised. The directions were simple: Find anything that looked like it was made out of plastic or nonnatural fibers. Why? Because one of the main raw materials used to make plastic goods is—you guessed it—petroleum. Oil-based polymers are everywhere. After about 15 minutes of looking Kela gasped, "Wow, Daddy, I didn't know we had so much oil in our house. We should open up a gas station!" It seems that everything we own has oil in it.

> Oil-based polymers are everywhere.

In fact, this is largely true. Almost every electric appliance has a polymer casing: TVs, power adapters, electric cords, cable and stereo boxes, and so forth. The circuit boards inside our electronic gadgets are also made from polymers. Here is a short list of the polymer-based items we found around the house:

Table 6.1 Embedded Fossil Fuels: A Mercer Island Example

1 each: soccer ball, basketball, beach ball
10 pairs of (old and moldy) running/sports shoes
6 snow boots
6 ski jackets
2 desks
30 Tupperware-like containers
4 chairs
10 sweaters
15 shirts
8 pairs of nylon pantyhose
1,000 square feet of nylon carpet
1 children's sled
Casing for all power tools
etc., etc.

Of course, the tally of my family's current possessions barely reflects our true environmental impact. What about all the old sneakers, broken toys, and other junk that we have used and thrown away over the years that are now rotting in some landfill? How about the polyester Scooby Doo comforter that used to grace Kela's bed? More oil!

Yes, our lives are awash in nonrenewable oil and other fossil fuel–based chemicals. In order to more precisely measure our impact, we also need to take into account the resources required to produce, transport, package, sell, and dispose of each product. This "embedded energy" makes up an important component of our contribution to climate change and is a factor to weigh in making informed consumer decisions. For example, you might assume your leather couch and shoes are OK compared to synthetic products. Wrong. Do you know how much oil it takes to raise a cow to maturity? Two hundred and eighty-three gallons (Appenzeller and Dimick, 2004)! Or, perhaps you are thinking of buying a new energy-saving Prius. Well, by some estimates, getting a typical auto through the production process and into the showroom generates more than 3,000 lb (1,362 kg) of carbon dioxide (Reay, 2005). Therefore, it may take a number of years for the environmental benefits associated with better gas mileage and partial zero emissions to make up for the environmental costs of production, distribution, and marketing.

With so many factors to consider, how can we make informed decisions as environmentally conscious consumers? One government-funded UK firm, The Carbon Trust, has embarked on a crusade to create a product labeling system that systematically quantifies total product cycle GHG emissions. These product cycle stages include raw material production, raw material transport, manufacturing, distribution and retailing, consumption, and disposal. The Carbon Trust has carried out a number of demonstration projects with corporate partners to prove that carbon footprint labeling is practical and desirable for consumers *and* producers. For instance, the organization recently completed a life cycle carbon analysis for potato chips made by Walkers, the UK's largest snack food producer. The study examined everything from potato production to cooking and distribution methods. Researchers found that the water content of potatoes varied significantly and was largely dependent on farmer land-use practices (less water use is better). They noted that different mixes of energy used in the production process (e.g., grid electricity

> How can we make informed decisions as environmentally conscious consumers?

vs. primary energy such as natural gas) had a big impact on emissions. The study also found that about one-third of emissions were linked to packaging. Overall, it concluded that changes to supply-chain processes could reduce emissions by 8% and save Walkers money (The Carbon Trust, 2006)

The Food We Eat: Comparative Climate Impacts

I hope that efforts by The Carbon Trust and similar groups will eventually take complexity and uncertainty out of climate dieting, especially when it comes to processed and packaged foods. Unfortunately, it could be years before reliable carbon labeling appears on store shelves. Also, there is still some uncertainty about how to factor distance traveled, or "food miles," into the equation (Murray, 2007). So what's a conscientious consumer to do? Luckily there are two categories of items we use every day where the science is clearer and our climate impact can be measured and controlled with relative ease: domestically produced raw and semiprocessed food and solid waste.

Table 6.2 provides selected per capita consumption patterns for basic food items in five OECD countries. The second column from the left provides the estimated amount of grams of carbon dioxide equivalent emissions associated with the production of 2.2 lb (1 kg) of a product. Multiply this number by the per capita consumption value for each product category to find the per capita climate impact for each type of food.

Our model home has four members. In this case, we use the U.S. numbers as a baseline (but you can pick any country for your own analysis), and UK consumption patterns as one possible option for where our model family may want to go when it comes to reducing food consumption impacts. Please note that grams of carbon dioxide equivalent used in this Danish study only apply to minimally processed foods and do not include packaging or marketing costs. The value for beef is for live cattle. For a more complete list of food items and their associated atmospheric effect go to Appendix F.

To better illustrate the effect of food on the climate, let's compare

Table 6.2 Food Consumption and GHG Emissions

Food Item	Grams CO_2e per kg/Product	U.S. (kg)	France (kg)	Italy (kg)	Spain (kg)	UK (kg)	kg CO_2 Product (U.S.)	kg CO_2 Product (UK)
Eggs (kg/year)	2,000	22.3	16.2	12.6	18.3	12.6	44.6	25.2
Dairy (kg/year)[a]	1,200	131	110	88	102	130	157.2	156.0
Rice (kg/year)	1,000	9.1	5.3	8.4	6.2	6.7	9.1	6.7
Beef (kg/year) (live)	11,600	28.6	28	25	15	15	331.8	174.0
Pork (kg/year) (ham shank)	2,950	21.7	38	39	65	16	64.0	47.2
Poultry (kg/year) (retail)	3,160	26.9	24	18	33	27	85.0	85.3
Fresh veg. (kg/year)	150	93	138	151	147	89	14.0	13.4
Subtotal, CO_2e produced for basic foods basket							705.7	507.8
Multiply # in household							4	4
Grand total for household (kg)							2,822.8	2,031.2
(lb)							6,210.2	4,468.6

Note: Figures for grams CO_2e for food production in Denmark. Actual values vary by country. CO_2 figures are for raw goods and generally do not take into account packaging, cooking, or processing. 1 kg = 2.2 lb. Consumption values are reported on a per capita basis.

[a] Grams CO_2e per kg/product is for milk, which is used as a proxy for all dairy products.

Source: U.S. consumption figures from U.S. Department of Agriculture (2005), www.usda.gov. European consumption figures are from European Commission Joint Research Centre (2005). *Energy, Lifestyles and Climate Technical Report*, European Commission, Brussels, Belgium.

two common meals. Meal one includes a nice round steak entrée, bakery-fresh bread, baked potatoes, buttered carrots and fried onions on the side, and two-liters of milk. For meal two, we swap the steak for a cod fillet.

Who would think that making this simple menu change could decrease your GHG emissions by more than 80%? Note that these numbers do not include energy used to prepare and cook the meal.

Before we run out to buy that cod fillet, we need to consider another issue. In the example in the table, substituting cod for steak substantially reduced the GHG emissions of our consumption. However, overfishing of wild cod has effectively transformed this formerly abundant species into a depleting resource. Switching to farm-raised fish does not necessarily improve the situation because most fish feed originates from unsustainable sources (e.g., genetically modified

Substituting cod for steak substantially reduced the GHG emissions of our consumption.

Table 6.3 Tale of Two Meals

Meal 1				Meal 2			
Food	kg	Grams CO$_2$e per kg/Product	Total Grams CO$_2$e	Food	kg	Grams CO$_2$e per kg/Product	Total Grams CO$_2$e
Steak tenderloin (round)	1	42,300	42,300	Cod (frozen-retail)	1	3,200	3,200
Potatoes	0.5	220	110	Potatoes	0.5	220	110
Bread (bakery)	0.5	780	390	Bread (bakery)	0.5	780	390
Milk (skim L)	2	1,200	2400	Milk (skim L)	2	1,200	2,400
Carrots	0.5	120	60	Carrots	0.2	120	24
Onions	0.5	380	190	Tomato	0.2	3,450	690
				Onions	0.2	380	76
Total							
kg			45.45				6.89
lb			99.99				15.16
CO$_2$e diff.[a]	kg	38.56					
	lb	84.83					

Note: Figures for grams CO$_2$e for food production in Denmark. Actual values vary by country.

Source: LCA Food Database (2006) www.lcafood.dk.

[a] difference

soybeans or wheat). Fish farms also generate enormous amounts of waste that can find its way into local water supplies if not managed correctly. Ask your grocer or farmers' market vendor where your fish came from, or buy fish that is certified (preferably by a government or an equivalent certifying agency) as originating from sustainably managed stocks. Better yet, you could just switch the fish for another protein source, such as organic tofu (620 g of GHG emissions produced per kg of soybeans).

Ask your grocer or farmers' market vendor where your fish came from.

More on the Environmental Cost of Meat Consumption

You may have noticed from our food consumption table that meat production emits huge amounts of GHGs. But this is just the beginning of the list of hazards that meat production potentially poses to the environment. Naturalist Jane Goodall (2005) in her book *Harvest for Hope: A Guide for Mindful Eating* eloquently describes the broader environmental, economic, and ethical impact of meat production. The costs of beef production are immense. In the United States, 56% of all farmland is dedicated to beef production. In the United Kingdom, about 70% of farmland is used to produce animals or the food they need to survive. The demand for feedstock is so high that most countries are now net importers of grain. Large multinationals have cleared tens of millions of acres of rain forests around the world to grow food to feed the cattle we eat. When you think of the sheer size of an Angus bull it is not difficult to understand why grain is in such demand. It takes 35 lb (16 kg) of grain to produce 2.2 lb (1 kg) of beef. Producing 1 lb (0.454 kg) of edible chicken takes more than 3.5 lb (1.6 kg) of feed. Also, producing 1 lb of beef requires 26,420 gal (100,000 L) of water; 1lb of chicken meat requires 13,247 gal (50,140 L; Goodall, 2005).

> In the United States, 56% of all farmland is dedicated to beef production.

Ever wondered why there are so many starving people in the world? Well, now you know one of the main reasons. Not surprisingly, Goodall is a strong advocate of vegetarianism. Reducing meat consumption is one of the best things we can do to alter our impact on the atmosphere and on Mother Nature's other scarce resources.

> Reducing meat consumption is one of the best things we can do to alter our impact on the atmosphere.

The Waste We Hide: Disposal and Recycling

One of the saddest things about our consumption is that much of what we buy never gets used at all. It is just thrown away. Elizabeth Royte's (2005) wonderful little book *Garbage Land: The Secret Trail of Trash* chronicles the adventures of our discarded excess and the devastating effect it has on the environment. How much trash do we throw into our garbage bins every day? Table 6.4 provides some numbers from

Table 6.4 **Waste Disposal and Recycling**

Waste	Current—Where You Are		Waste		Future—Where You Want to Be			
	Per Person	Per Person		Per Person	Per Person	Per Person	Per Person	Per Person
	Waste/day	Waste/yr	Type	CO_2/yr	Waste/yr	CO_2/yr	Waste/yr	CO_2/yr
	2003 (lb)	2003 (lb)		2003 (lb)	60% recycled (lb)	60% recycled (lb)	25% cut (lb)	25% cut (lb)
Total	4.45	1,624.25		1,940.0	1,624.25	1,461.83	1,218.2	1,096.4
Recycle	1.04	379.6	23%	248.2	974.55	487.28	730.9	365.5
Compost	0.32	116.8	7%					
Discard	3.09	1,127.85	69%	1,691.8	649.7	974.55	487.3	730.9
Subtotal	4.45	1,624.25	100%	1,940.0	1,624.25	1,461.83	1,218.2	1,096.4
Number in household	4	4		4	4	4	4	4
Total	17.8	6,497		7,759.9	6,497	5,847.30	4,872.8	4,385.5
					(lb)	(kg)		
CO_2e reduction from 60% recycling					1,912.6	867.54		
CO_2e reduction from 60% recycling and 25% cut in waste					3,374.4	1,530.61		

Note: Values for U.S. only. EPA (2003) municipal solid waste (MSW) pounds per day 1 lb recycling = 0.5 lb CO_2e 1 lb landfill waste = 1.5 lb CO_2e. Figures are calculated for 365-day year. 60% recycling is carried out first, followed by a 25% reduction in each waste type. Visit www.climatediet.com/tables.asp to compute your own values.

Composting value combined with recycling for CO_2 calculations.

the United States. Americans are at the top of the heap when it comes to trash. Therefore, these values almost certainly overstate waste production in other countries. Unfortunately, good comparative numbers are hard to come by.

In 2003 per capita trash disposal clocked in at 4.45 lb per day, or 1,624 lb (737 kg) per year. Unfortunately, more than two-thirds of this went straight into landfills. Some form of household recycling is mandatory in Japan and in most EU countries but not in many parts of North America. Most landfill waste is totally unnecessary because most trash has recyclable elements. The benefits of recycling are manifold, but I would like to focus on just one. On average, landfill waste generates about 1.5 lb of GHG emissions versus 0.5 lb for recycled trash (EPA, 2003; Gershon, 2006). What happens if our model family increases its recycling rate to 60%? Emissions drop by more than 1,900 lb (862.6 kg). If you take the bold move of actually reducing trash production by 25% by cutting down on purchases of heavily packaged goods (can you say individually wrapped snack packs?), we can cut our GHG emissions by an additional 1,462 lb (663.8 kg).

✓   Adopting UK-like eating habits reduces our model family's emissions by 28% to 4,468.6 lb (2028.7 kg) of carbon dioxide equivalent. Or, if you think you can top UK consumers, put in your own values. You just won a Bronze Medal.

✓   Increasing waste recycling to 60% reduces carbon dioxide equivalent emissions by more than 1,900 lb (862.6 kg).

✓   Cutting total household waste production reduces emissions by an additional 1,462 lb (663.8 kg). Overall, increasing recycling and reducing waste will decrease emissions by 43% and win you a Bronze Medal!

Composting for the Planet

There is no better way to get rid of our own waste than to take responsibility for returning our leftovers to where they came from—the land. Disposing of our own food waste—by composting—reduces GHGs associated with waste disposal even more than disposal company recycling. By composting when possible, we replace all the unsustainable processes related to the corporate disposal of waste: the garbage hauler, garbage truck, distribution and sorting centers, and landfills.

In 2003 per capita trash disposal clocked in at 4.45 lb per day.

There is no better way to get rid of our own waste than to take responsibility for returning our leftovers to where they came from—the land.

"Composting is a method of solid-waste management whereby the organic (formerly living) component of the solid waste stream is biologically decomposed under controlled conditions to produce a valuable end product" (Washington State Department of Ecology, 2005, pp. 2–3). The goal is simple. Composting helps along Mother Nature's eons-long process of taking organic matter and decomposing it into its constituent parts so it can be reused. Compost alleviates the need for chemical-based fertilizers by acting as a repository for the slow release of plant nutrients. Compost also acts as a carbon sink, because it returns GHGs to the soil where they belong, rather than allowing them to quickly slip into the atmosphere.

Compost alleviates the need for chemical-based fertilizers.

Table 6.5 contains a list of things that can or cannot be composted.

Table 6.5 What You Can Compost

OK to Compost	Not OK to Compost
Grass clippings	Meat and dairy products
Spent flowers	Weed seeds/diseased plants
Shredded or dried leaves	Highly invasive weeds
Moss	Poisonous plants
Shredded newspaper or cardboard	Weed and feed products
Vegetable peels	Black walnut leaves
Coffee grounds	Pet waste
Fruit peels, waste	Human waste
Bread scraps	Glossy paper
Farm animal manure	Chemically treated wood
Hair	Wood ash
Shredded broadleaf evergreens	Lime
Shredded pine needles	Compost starter/fertilizer
Straw	Soil
Chipped branches	Sand
Pinecones	Oily/greasy kitchen waste
Shredded natural fabrics	Fresh broadleaf evergreens
Sod	Any other stuff that is not organic (e.g., daughter's Barbie doll)

Source: Washington State Department of Ecology (2004).

How can you join the composting revolution? Let's look at an example that shows us how we can process organic food waste. First, install a receptacle in a strategic place in your kitchen that can be dedicated to organic food waste. Second, get a composting container. You can use any sturdy container or you can purchase a dedicated composter from a local vendor. The vendor containers often come packaged in a kit, complete with directions, worms, and so on, and run between $50 to $100. Yes, I did say worms. One method of composting, called vermicomposting, involves placing red worms in bins with organic matter; the worms break down the matter into high-value compost. Worms are great recyclers because they eat almost anything. If you want to try this, you need to be aware of one thing. As with any other cold-blooded animal, worms are sensitive to climate changes. Temperatures ranging from 55° F to 77° F (13° C to 25° C) are ideal (EPA, 2007).

The Benefits of Buying Locally

A heated debate is making the rounds about the relative benefits of buying locally grown food—it makes intuitive sense that local products should be more climate friendly. One would expect that producing and transporting melons 10 miles should take far less energy than importing them from Mexico or New Zealand. However, the Walkers potato chip example discussed on p. 87 illustrated that food miles is just one small part of the picture. It is important to look at the entire life cycle: raw material production, raw material transport, manufacturing, distribution and retailing, consumption, and disposal. For instance, a study by New Zealand's Lincoln University concluded that dairy and lamb production was far more efficient in that country than in the United Kingdom. Therefore, the authors asserted, New Zealand products had a smaller overall climate impact than their equivalents that were locally produced in the United Kingdom. Another report from the UK's Manchester School of Business that examined the relative environmental impacts of 150 different items came to a similar conclusion (Murray, 2007).

Local farmers counter that these types of studies tout so-called efficient farming models while ignoring factors such as fossil fuel–based fertilizer use, chemical contamination from insecticides and herbicides, and the benefits of sustainable land-management practices. Increasingly, local farming means organic farming. Organic farming is more labor intensive, by necessity, than corporate farming, which is one of the aspects of organic food that many of us find most appealing. We are attracted to the idea that real people produced the food that sustains us with their own hands. We also like the sense of community associated with organic production, especially when the produce is sold at local farmers' markets. Organic farmers serve as conduits between city dwellers and the natural world, giving urbanites an opportunity to connect with rural life. Every time I shop at a farmers' market, I learn something new. Vendors are quick to dole out advice about the best time to plant spinach or keep weed growth down in our backyard garden. My daughter loves to wander through these markets, dazzled by the cornucopia of fresh produce. Also, few can argue that locally grown produce is fresher than its imported brethren.

> Organic farmers serve as conduits between city dwellers and the natural world.

Buying locally has another added benefit: It helps to preserve local culture and puts more of your hard-earned dollars, pounds, or yen to work in the local community. Corporate farming has driven the small family-owned farm to near oblivion. In the United States, less than 1% of workers identify farming as their primary occupation. Whether you go to supermarkets such as Safeway, Whole Foods, or Tesco to buy a pint of blackberries, most of the revenue generated from that sale takes a one-way path out of your hometown and into the coffers of overpaid executives and nameless shareholders who couldn't care less about the state of local schools, rising crime rates, or whether children have parks to play in. Local farmers care because they live among us. They send their kids to the same schools, shop in the same stores, and attend the same churches we do.

> Corporate farming has driven the small family-owned farm to near oblivion.

One more reason to buy locally is that it increases the likelihood that the organic products you buy are *actually* organic and healthier. Most local farmers are organized into self-regulating cooperatives. If market vendors misrepresent the products they sell, it is very likely that someone will call them on it. Also, local government food inspection controls and regimes are usually far more stringent than those applied to imported products. This fact was aptly illustrated in the United States in 2007 when imported Chinese grain laced with melamine was used in pet food and has been blamed for killing thousands of domestic dogs and cats. The U.S. government largely leaves inspection of imported foodstuffs in the hands of private industry (Heavey, 2007).

Personally I have a lot more confidence and trust in local organic farmers than in some nameless multinational corporation in guarding the quality of the food I feed my family. If local farmers mess up the environment, they themselves suffer the consequences. They have every incentive to treat the land with respect, use resources more responsibly, and avoid chemical use. They are also much more likely to treat their animals humanely. Corporate animal husbandry practices often inflict great suffering on those animals unfortunate enough to be caught in its clutches. For instance, most poultry is raised in "battery farms" where cages are stacked one on top of another, with four to six hens crammed together in each cage. Pigs are corralled in cages so narrow they cannot even turn around. Growth hormones are pumped into each animal to speed its dim march to the slaughterhouse. I think many of us would prefer not to support these types of practices (Goodall, 2005).

The Perils of Packaging

Regardless of whether you buy local or imported food, the fact remains that some types of food have a bigger impact on GHG emissions than others. Beef production is far more environmentally damaging than growing potatoes. On the whole, vegetable production has a smaller atmospheric impact than producing meat. And, recycled or not, packaged goods generally have bigger life cycle GHGs than food that is not packaged.

Many so-called green producers still do not understand these basic concepts. Case in point: coffee retailers. An increasing number of premium coffee vendors tout their fair trade, organically grown coffees. A certain segment of the coffee-drinking market, myself included, likes the idea that farmers are making a few extra cents on the dollar for every 500 g coffee bag sold (on average only one cent of every dollar generated at the retail level goes to farmers; fair trade increases the share to about a nickel). But the Mylar packaging that retailers often use is the pits when you factor in cradle-to-grave costs. But that is OK because of the happy buzz we feel when we drink our organic bitter Ethiopian roast, right?

Gift Giving

Our conscientious shopping decisions don't end at the grocery store or local coffeehouse. Gift giving is a huge part of most cultures, particularly during the winter holiday season. These days it seems that parents, spouses, and friends are increasingly engaged in an all-out battle to one-up each other on the gift-giving ladder. For instance, between Thanksgiving and New Year's, Americans generate more than one million extra tons of trash per week (Snohomish County Public Works, 2004).

It is now time to call a truce in the packaged gift-giving wars. I can hear many of you thinking "OK, I understand that we all need to save the atmosphere. But don't ruin my Christmas!" No one is asking you to stop giving. All I am suggesting is that you think creatively about strategies to give that are more environmentally responsible.

There are plenty of ways to express your affection for others without contributing to the destruction of old-growth forests (wrapping paper and packaging), sucking oil out of the ground (plastics and transportation), or adding to the mountains of trash that are already our legacy to our children. Here are some nice gift alternatives that will reflect your love and friendship for others while minimizing your contribution to climate change:

> *It is now time to call a truce in the packaged gift-giving wars.*

- ✓ Give experience/service gift certificates. Promise someone you love a week's worth of household chores, an evening of babysitting, an exercise club membership, or zoo or art museum tickets.

- ✓ If you give something made with nonrenewable materials, make sure you buy something that will last. Sports equipment or other items that encourage a healthy, active lifestyle are a good choice.

- ✓ Give gifts that will increase your loved one's appreciation for living a more climate-friendly lifestyle, such as environmental group memberships, compost bins, or gardening tools.

✓   Create your own personalized artwork—cards, books, pictures—
     using recycled materials or in electronic formats.

✓   Donate money in the name of your friend or neighbor to worthy
     causes like food banks, arts organizations, environmental groups,
     or animal shelters.

✓   Give gifts that are easy to recycle or reuse. Better yet, think about
     giving some really nice used clothes or other items.

✓   Avoid wrapping paper. If you must wrap, reuse existing
     paper around your house, such as old maps, shopping bags,
     calendars, gift bags or boxes, or old greeting cards or envelopes
     (Newdream, 2005).

Give gifts that are
easy to recycle or
reuse.

One final note on giving. If you have a gift recipient who either does
not understand your changing preferences in giving or just likes the old
way of doing things, don't rock the boat (or rock it *slowly*). Christmas
morning or a birthday party may not be the best time to introduce your
elderly parents to presents wrapped in recycled pages of the *Financial
Times*. But whatever you do, don't use environmentalism as an excuse
to *not* show your affection for others. If you don't think your loved ones
can handle changes in gift-giving customs, just go with the flow, and
make up for it by cutting your climate impact in other areas of your life.

Will Shopping Less Increase Unemployment?

If you look at the countries of origin for all of those cheap shoes, toys,
and sundries that bless the shelves of the average Jusco, Carrefour, or
Wal-Mart superstore, one thing will become immediately obvious: Most
of these cheap throwaway products are made in the developing world,
particularly in China. The majority of the plastic-molded toys we buy
for our children are made in small Chinese factories that have few or
no environmental safeguards (Chinese environmental laws look good
on paper but are poorly enforced). These factories are built along rivers
because it makes dumping trash and toxic waste much easier. China has
some of the dirtiest waterways in the world. Labor is cheap, but far more
energy is used per unit of output than in the United States, Canada, or
the United Kingdom (Harrington, 2005). Factor in the amount of energy

used to transport final products from their country of origin, and the dark side of these cheap products becomes apparent.

What about those nylon American flags that fly off the shelves like hotcakes around Independence Day in the United States? Many are made in China. Maybe retailers should be selling Chinese flags instead. But is it Wal-Mart's or Target's fault alone that Chinese-made goods are in such high demand? Not by a long shot. Consumers can choose how they want to spend their money. If Americans demand American-made toys, Wal-Mart would be sure to stock them. Buying locally made products will not put the Wal-Marts of the world out of business. They will adjust if consumers demand it.

Instead of importing everything, why can't we just make more products at home? As energy prices continue to increase, products that use fewer nonrenewable inputs and are more durable should become more price competitive. Instead of buying a cheap $10 imported coffeemaker every other year, why not buy a locally manufactured item that is built to last? If quality was more important to consumers, they might buy more products made in their own countries, which would stimulate rather than harm local employment. If consumers start caring about quality, durability, and recyclability, manufacturers and retailers will follow.

If consumers start caring about quality, durability, and recyclability, manufacturers and retailers will follow.

Outdoor Recreation and the Environment

One other form of consumption many of us engage in that we might want to keep an eye on is the use of recreational off-road vehicles and watercraft. I know how much fun it can be to speed through the forest on a snowmobile or do wheelies in sand dunes with an ATV. But off-road vehicle and recreational boat engines are far more polluting than automobiles or even diesel trucks. In the United States, the federal government did not even begin to regulate small recreational vehicle engine emissions until a few years ago. Traditional two-stroke engines that were once a mainstay in the recreational vehicle market dump 25% to 30% of their oil-gas fuel mixture unburned into the air and water. Unburned fuel contains a host of toxic chemicals including Methyl tertiary-butyl ether (MTBE), benzene, and formaldehyde. Newer four-stroke engines reduce this threat but are still quite inefficient. Additional problems posed by off-road vehicles include noise pollution and habitat destruction. In 2006 off-road vehicle users made more than 12 million visits to national parks and grasslands. One ATV speeding through a mountain meadow can do more damage than hundreds of individual hikers. High noise levels heap unnecessary stress on native species and hikers alike (Natural Trails and Water Coalition, 2007; *Tucson Citizen*, 2007).

The next time you visit the great outdoors, consider leaving your ATV or dirt bike at home. Few things are more exhilarating than experiencing the natural world by foot; untethered by the technology and worries of modern life. To really become one with the biosphere, you must meet it on its own terms, not intrude on its inner workings by tearing up the landscape or scaring away every creature in sight.

My grandmother taught me the finer points of connecting with nature on foot. Grandma Harrington's favorite leisure activity was flower collecting. Each summer she took me up into the hills above Yakima, WA, along the eastern slopes of the Cascades to walk the high mountain meadows, searching for the perfect blooms for her pressed flower collection. Under the bright summer sun, these meadows were a sunburst of color, with green, white, and purple hues. Bees floated lazily by, spreading the nectar of life everywhere they went. Snow-tipped peaks beckoned above us. She knew the name of every flower, every tree, every bird. Along the way, we would stop at a mountain lodge to feast on fresh trout. What a delicacy!

Next time you visit the great outdoors, consider leaving your ATV or dirt bike at home.

Just Consume Less

There is really only one surefire way to escape the detrimental effects of modern consumption—consume less. And when we do partake, we should try to choose products that have the smallest environmental impact. Purchasing products that are longer lasting, have less packaging, use sustainably produced materials, can be reused and recycled, and have lower transportation costs will usually decrease your climate footprint. Instead of taking the kids on a trip to the mall or racing through forest thickets on dirt bikes, why not enjoy an evening at home or a leisurely

Don't let marketers and advertisers run your life.

walk along your favorite nature trail? Reconnect with your family. Talk with your spouse or significant other. Don't let marketers and advertisers run your life. Take control. And save the atmosphere as well.

Tips Summary

Model home changes for food and waste zones:

✓ Reduce consumption of meat and increase consumption of less GHG-intensive foods such as fish and vegetables.

✓ Increase recycling rate to 60% and reduce total garbage volume by 25%.

For even more savings:

✓ Avoid overly packaged food products.

✓ Consider reducing or eliminating consumption of meat, especially red meat.

✓ Buy locally produced organic products.

✓ Avoid nonseasonal foods that require significant shipping (e.g., Chilean grapes in winter).

✓ Frequent farmers' markets.

✓ Compost more often.

✓ Avoid animal husbandry products raised using inhumane rearing practices.

✓ Use products made from sustainably harvested or recycled materials.

✓ Give nonmaterial gifts, reduce use of wrapping paper and other packaging.

✓ Just buy less stuff. Spend less time shopping.

✓ Leave your recreational vehicles at home.

Hit the Road the Climatewise Way

.7

Our Love Affair With the Automobile

Our love affair with the automobile—the venerable child of the industrial age—has lasted for more than a century. Since Henry Ford first popularized the notion of mass private car ownership, few possessions have been more symbolic of individual freedom. Remember the first time you sat behind the wheel of one of these great contraptions, fearful but excited? The rumble of the engine quickened as you placed your foot on the accelerator. Or perhaps you recall the sound of screeching rubber as you struggled to tame the massive beast into submission. Getting that first driver's license ranks among the most important events in many people's lives. That little laminated scrap of paper represents the ticket to a new way of life, a rite of passage from adolescence to adulthood.

Unfortunately, a dark reality underlies our love affair with the car. Virtually all vehicles sold in the developed world run on nonrenewable fossil fuels. In the United States, personal car and truck use has become so ubiquitous that there are more cars per household (1.9) than people (1.8). Yet, while vehicle ownership has proliferated, fuel efficiency has stagnated. Despite continued technological advances in the overall economy, by 2007 the average fuel economy of American vehicles had barely budged from its 1980s' level of about 23–24 miles per gallon (mpg). Other nations have made somewhat more progress in improving automobile efficiency. Developing countries China and India have car fuel efficiency standards above 30 mpg (World Changing, 2007). EU rates are also much higher. However, the fact remains that more than 98% of vehicles on the road worldwide still run on fossil fuels, as opposed to biodiesel or other alternatives.

In the United States there are more cars per household (1.9) than people (1.8).

These two trends create a dangerous combination that threatens the atmosphere, OECD economies, and national security. President Bush's "we are addicted to oil" refrain resonated with the American public in the months following Hurricane Katrina, when average gas prices topped $3 per gallon (Bumiller and Nagourney, 2006). How big is this addiction? In 2006 the United States used more than 20 million barrels of oil per day (bpd). Of this amount, more than 60% was imported. Forty percent of this value was used for—you guessed it— personal vehicles. If the United States continues with business as usual, consumption could increase to between 26 million and 33 million bpd by 2025 (EIA, 2005).

Where is all of this oil going to come from? Not from most developed nations. Even with new extraction technologies, U.S. and European reserves are peaking or are in decline. Canadian production is increasing, but this is partly driven by the removal of oil from tar sands, which is far more polluting than traditional oil extraction methods. Therefore, most production increases will come mainly from the Middle East, Russia, or other potentially unstable parts of the world. Each time Iran threatens to expand its nuclear program or an Iraqi or Saudi oil field is attacked by terrorists, oil prices gyrate, sending stock markets into a tailspin and putting upward pressure on interest rates. Also, no matter where the oil comes from, as long as we keep using more of it, GHG emissions will continue to increase (Gelbspan, 2004).

Obviously, something has to give. One thing is certain. These problems did not appear overnight, nor have the powers that be—the oil and auto industries and governments—been aggressive enough to change this state of affairs. No, we cannot wait around for government to fix our love affair with the combustion engine. If we are going to reach the 70% plus GHG emissions reductions necessary to stabilize the climate by 2050, we all need to take matters into our own hands.

We cannot wait around for government to fix our love affair with the combustion engine.

The High Cost of Private Car Ownership

Our car envy comes at a steep price. We have already chronicled how climate change is afflicting vulnerable populations around the world. Unfortunately, markets are very poor at adequately internalizing the total economic costs of these environmental externalities. However, let's try to come up with some real numbers that quantify the environmental and economic costs of auto ownership.

The European Union mandates that large GHG polluting firms pay additional taxes and fees if their emissions are above certain predetermined levels. The largest carbon dioxide market in the world, the European Climate Exchange, is in the business of quantifying the right to emit one metric ton of carbon dioxide. In March 2007 one metric ton of carbon dioxide was valued at about 17.50 Euros for December 2008 contracts, or $23.27 (European Climate Exchange,

2007). In the United States, this cost is not yet directly paid by the polluter, but it is paid by society (through degradation and depletion of natural resources). Furthermore, this dollar value greatly underestimates the effect of emissions on regional and global ecosystems. However, the Climate Exchange does provide a starting point for quantifying the economic value of carbon dioxide equivalent emissions (Point Carbon, 2007). Climate-conscious consumers may want to consider including this carbon cost in the operating expenses of their vehicles. You can do this either by purchasing carbon offset contracts directly from the European Climate Exchange or from a private vendor.

If You Must Buy . . . Tips

If you must buy a vehicle, what factors should you consider to evaluate the environmental and economic impacts of your purchase? Table 7.1 provides a list of vehicles by class sold in the U.S. market in 2007. The table is split into three sections: The first section lists the most energy-efficient vehicles by class. The second and third sections contrast examples from the other side of the efficiency equation: luxury autos and big SUVs. Obviously, models vary by year and market and they change frequently. So our purpose here is not to recommend specific vehicles, but to illustrate how different consumer choices can affect the climate, and your pocketbook.

Among the most efficient vehicles, the Toyota Prius has the lowest fuel use and yearly emissions (258 gal/5,160 lb carbon dioxide [976.5 L/2,341 kg]). At $3 per gallon, yearly gasoline costs run about $774 per year. Purchasing carbon offsets (see chapter 8) adds an additional $40–$50 to your bill. Among nonhybrids, the Toyota Yaris does best ($1,146/382 gal/7,640 lb carbon dioxide [1,446 L/3,465 kg]) followed by the Honda Fit small station wagon ($1,209/403 gal/8,060 lb carbon dioxide [1,525L/3,656 kg]). Operating a minivan like a Dodge Caravan that gets an average of around 20 mpg consumes more than twice the fuel as the hybrid model ($1,839/613 gal/12,260 lb carbon dioxide [2,320 L/5,561 kg]). Finally, a typical large SUV like the Ford Expedition will consume 850 gal (3,217 L), run you $2,550, and emit 17,000 lb (7,711 kg) of carbon dioxide.

A Dodge Caravan that gets an average of around 20 mpg consumes more than twice the fuel as the hybrid model.

Table 7.1 Comparative Financial and Environmental Costs of Private Vehicles (2007)

Vehicle Category	Transmission	Class	mpg City	mpg Hwy	gal/yr	CO₂/yr (lb)	CO₂/yr (kg)	$3.00 Gallon[a]	$6.00 Gallon[b]
Best mpg/Class (Auto)									
Mini Cooper	Auto	Minicompact	22	30	480	9,600	4,354	1,440	2,880
Toyota Yaris	Auto	Subcompact	29	35	382	7,640	3,465	1,146	2,292
Civic Hybrid	Auto	Compact	40	45	285	5,700	2,585	855	1,710
Toyota Prius Hybrid	Auto	Midsize	48	45	258	5,160	2,341	774	1,548
Honda Accord	Auto	Large	21	31	488	9,760	4,427	1,464	2,928
Honda Fit	Auto	Station wagon	27	34	403	8,060	3,656	1,209	2,418
VW Passat	Auto	Midsize wagon	20	28	523	10,460	4,745	1,569	3,138
Toyota Tacoma 2WD	Auto	Standard pickup	19	25	563	11,260	5,107	1,689	3,378
Dodge Caravan	Auto	Minivan	17	24	613	12,260	5,561	1,839	3,678
Ford Escape Hybrid 4WD	Auto	SUV	34	30	374	7,480	3,393	1,122	2,244
Money Is No Object									
Ferrari F430	Auto	Two seat	11	16	938	18,760	8,509	2,814	5,628
Mercedes Maybach 62	Auto	Large	10	16	998	19,960	9,054	2,994	5,988
Hummer H-3 3.7L	Auto	SUV	14	18	771	15,420	6,994	2,313	4,626
Maserati Quattroporte	Auto	Large	13	19	792	15,840	7,185	2,376	4,752
Big SUVs									
Ford Expedition	Auto	SUV	12	18	850	17,000	7,711	2,550	5,100
Cadillac Escalade	Auto	SUV	12	19	834	16,680	7,566	2,502	5,004
BMW X5 4.8i	Auto	SUV	15	21	697	13,940	6,323	2,091	4,182
Lexus LX570	Auto	SUV	12	18	850	17,000	7,711	2,550	5,100

Note: All examples are based on use of regular unleaded gasoline. Some high-performance autos require the use of premium (higher octane fuels). Model names are for the U.S. market. Model names may vary by country. This study uses the EPA new mileage rating system that tests cars based on more realistic driving conditions. The standard used to compute mileage in the European Union and the United States differs slightly so mileage values presented here are not exactly comparable to EU publications. However, in most cases measurement differences vary no more than +/− 10%. One U.S. gal = 3.785 L.

Source: EPA (2007b), Fuel Economy Guide: Model Year 2008, available at www.fueleconomy.gov/feg/FEG2000.htm.

[a] Annual fuel cost at $3.00/gallon; [b] annual fuel cost at $6.00/gallon.

And what happens if, God forbid, the price of gas goes to $4 or $6 per gallon? At $6 per gallon, the cost of ownership increases by thousands of dollars more. Japanese, UK, and German drivers are well aware of this. In 2003 the median metro Seattle household income was about $48,000 per year before taxes. Can you imagine paying more than $10,000 after tax dollars (two Expeditions) just for fuel?

When you add depreciation, maintenance, and insurance, many families end up spending more on their vehicles than on their mortgages or their children's college educations. If you want to get a better handle on the total cost of ownership (TCO), visit www.edmunds.com/apps/cto/CTOintroController (calculations apply to the U.S. market only). This Web site provides fairly accurate TCO estimates for virtually every vehicle on the road. When I checked out the numbers for a new version of our last vehicle, I was shocked to find out just how expensive it was to keep our little steel friend around. The breakdown is presented in Table 7.2.

> Many families end up spending more on their vehicles than on their mortgages.

Though it may seem heretical to the way many of us live—with our two- and three-car garages—consider whether your household can function with just one vehicle. Using Edmunds's historical numbers, I estimate that Kathy and I have saved more than $100,000 over the 18 years of our marriage because of our choice to get by with one car and use public transportation more frequently. That is a substantial amount of money, even more so if you calculate the compounded value over time. Assuming a 5% yearly rate of return, that little nest egg will grow to a whopping $338,000 over 25 years. I do not know about you, but that is a big chunk of change for our family (go to http://cgi.money.cnn.com/tools/savingscalc/savingscalc.html to calculate your savings). Again, this calculator does not even take into account the social and environmental savings associated with decreasing private vehicle use.

> Consider whether your household can function with just one vehicle.

Table 7.2 True Cost to Own a 2007 Volvo

Expense Category	Year 1	Year 2	Year 3	Year 4	Year 5		5-Year Total
Depreciation	$9,782	$4,900	$4,313	$3,822	$3,429		$26,246
Financing	$2,999	$2,429	$1,811	$1,141	$416		$8,796
Insurance	$1,571	$1,626	$1,683	$1,708	$1,803		$8,391
Taxes & fees	$3,448	$50	$50	$50	$50		$3,648
Fuel	$1,910	$1,967	$2,026	$2,087	$2,150		$10,140
Maintenance	$151	$731	$483	$1,129	$1,095		$3,589
Repairs	$0	$0	$0	$575	$881		$1,456
Yearly Totals	$19,861	$11,703	$10,366	$10,512	$9,824		$62,266

Note: Values are for U.S. market. Model is the base Volvo S-80 2.9.

Source: Edmunds (2007).

New Versus Used

When it comes to selecting your family's vehicles, there is also the new-versus-used debate. From a purely financial perspective, purchasing a new car is almost always more expensive than buying a used one because of depreciation. On average, new cars lose more than 25% of their value during the first year of ownership. Buying used is also often the best choice from a GHG standpoint as well. Why? Whenever you purchase a new car, you are signaling the marketplace that there is demand for new vehicles, which encourages manufacturers to increase production. And more production means more emissions. In contrast, used vehicles are already on the road—buying one is less likely to encourage new-car production. The main exception to this rule is when a new car offers a substantially higher mpg (or km/L) rating than available used vehicles. For instance, when hybrids came on the market a few years ago, their energy-use characteristics were so much better than what was available at the time that their multiyear emissions savings were greater than the embedded energy associated with their manufacture.

It is important to note that the most fuel-efficient hybrids will not meet the needs of every family. Hybrid selection in each vehicle classification is extremely limited. If you have more than five people in your family and want to get by with one car, none of the small hybrids available in 2007 is a practical choice. Also, hybrids still command a price premium of $3,000–$10,000 (or more in Europe) over similar nonhybrid cars. So, as a general rule of thumb, simply try to purchase the smallest and most fuel-efficient vehicle that will meet your needs.

> Try to purchase the smallest and most fuel-efficient vehicle that will meet your needs.

Getting More Out of What You Have

In most cases, the best way to save money and the atmosphere is to get more out of what you have. Here is a list of tips you might want to consider in making optimal use of your existing vehicles:

✓ If you don't drive, you will not burn gas. Decreasing overall auto use is the best way to cut emissions and preserve the useful life of your vehicle. Consider combining small trips or carpooling or using public transportation (discussed later in the chapter).

✓ Drive conservatively. Aggressive driving, including hard acceleration and braking, can reduce gas mileage by as much at 33%. Accelerate slowly from a full stop and drive near the speed limit. For every 5 mph you drive over 60 mph (95 km/h), efficiency declines by 10%.

✓ Use the recommended grade of motor oil for your vehicle and keep tires properly inflated—this can improve fuel economy by 5%.

✓ Regularly take your car in for a tune-up and replace air filters when needed. These actions can increase your mileage by an additional 4%.

✓ Avoid idling your vehicle. Idling cars get 0 mpg (km/L). If you find yourself sitting in congestion for more than 30 seconds, you will save gas by turning off the engine and then restarting it when traffic starts moving.

✓ Close windows and sunroofs and remove other items that might reduce the aerodynamic characteristics of your vehicle.

Remove extra weight from your vehicle. Each 100 extra pounds can reduce gas mileage by 2% (Daily Fuel Economy, 2007; EPA, 2007b; European Commission, DG Environment, 2006).

Public or Human-Powered Transportation: The Clean and Cheap Alternative

There is a better path toward greener mobility. Those of us who live in urban and suburban communities can use public transportation, which is more than 90% more climate friendly than private automobiles (and is almost always less expensive). Most people who live in temperate climates cannot live without lights or hot water. But the great bulk of us could easily get by without owning a car. Millions of us do. However, most of us do not.

> The great bulk of us could easily get by without owning a car.

Let's look at the comparative impact on the atmosphere of different forms of public transportation. Table 7.3a and Table 7.3b list GHG emissions by conveyance type and are computed based on a usage rate of 12,000 miles (19,312 km) per year, which is typical in the highest per capita carbon-emitting countries. Before beginning this discussion, let me give one caveat: Numerous factors can influence the environmental effects of each of these transportation types. Vehicle occupancy, speed, engine characteristics, fuel used, fuel mix used for electricity generation, country of manufacture, and environmental characteristics all influence climate impacts. However, previous studies provide average cross-national values for transport types. While they might not exactly reflect your own community situation, they do illustrate how each public transportation mode roughly compares to others.

According to EU statistics, among these different modes of urban public transportation, bus use generates the least amount of per capita carbon dioxide emissions. Trailing the bus slightly is the subway, which generates 665 lb (302 kg) of carbon dioxide per person per 12,000 miles (19,312 km) traveled. Not surprisingly, taxi travel is the least environmentally friendly form of public transport.

> Taxi travel is the least environmentally friendly form of public transport.

We can use the transportation worksheet to calculate the effects of using public transport on the climate. Our old scenario reflects

Table 7.3a Transportation Zone Worksheet (U.S. Miles)

Transport Type	CO₂/yr (lb) 12,000 mi	Current—Where You Are		Future—Where You Want to Be		
		Mile/yr	CO₂/yr (lb)	Mile/yr	CO₂/yr (lb)	Diff.[a]
Public						
Bus	466	0.0	0.0	4,000.0	155.3	-155.3
Train	791	0.0	0.0	4,000.0	263.7	-263.7
Subway	665	0.0	0.0	2,000.0	110.8	-110.8
Boat	1,100	0.0	0.0	1,000.0	91.7	-91.7
Airplane	9,360	6,000.0	4,680.0	6,000.0	4,680.0	0.0
Taxi	11,380	0.0	0.0	0.0	0.0	0.0
Tram	1,424	0.0	0.0	0.0	0.0	0.0
Trolley	1,266	0.0	0.0	1,000.0	105.5	-105.5
Total Public		**6,000.0**	**4,680.0**	**18,000.0**	**5,407.0**	**-727.0**
Private						
Bicycle	228	0.0	0.0	0.0	0.0	0.0
Prius	5,160	0.0	0.0	0.0	0.0	0.0
Honda Fit	8,060	0.0	0.0	0.0	0.0	0.0
Honda Accord	9,760	12,000.0	9,760.0	0.0	0.0	9,760.0
Caravan	12,260	12,000.0	12,260.0	12,000.0	12,260.0	0.0
Expedition	17,000	0.0	0.0	0.0	0.0	0.0
Yours?	0	0.0	0.0	0.0	0.0	0.0
Total Private		**24,000.0**	**22,020.0**	**12,000.0**	**12,260.0**	**9,760.0**
Total All		**30,000.0**	**26,700.0**	**30,000.0**	**17,667.0**	**9,033.0**

Notes: Each gallon burned emits 20 lb of CO_2 (9.072 kg). Your CO_2 = (gallons used/year) x 20. Visit www.fueleconomy.gov or similar for gallons/year. Visit www.climatediet.com/tables.asp to calculate own values.

CO_2 per year = (CO_2/12,000 mi). One mi = 1.609344 km.12,000 mi/year (19,312.1 km).

Values may vary significantly based on speed, occupancy, and size of transport.

Public transport figures based on EU averages and reflect use per capita and average urban occupancy rate. Taxi value assumes one passenger occupancy. Bus, subway, and trolley rates denote urban, not long-haul use.

[a] difference

Sources: European Commission Joint Research Center (2005). Jet emissions from Terrapass.com (2007) and European Commission, DG Environment (2005a).

the transportation choices of a typical two-car suburban household. Private vehicle use generates more than 22,000 lbs (8,710 kg) of carbon dioxide per year. A yearly family plane trip to grandma's house adds an additional 4,680 lbs (2,123 kg). Now, let's look at what happens if that same household replaces 12,000 mi of driving with an equal amount of public transport. **Total emissions drop by more than 9,000 lbs (4,086 kg), which is almost equivalent to the climate impact of heating our**

Table 7.3b **Transportation Zone Worksheet (Metric)**

Transport Type	CO₂/yr (kg) 19,312 km	Current—Where You Are		Future—Where You Want to Be		
		km/yr	CO₂/yr (kg)	km/yr	CO₂/yr (kg)	Diff.ᵃ
Public						
Bus	211	0.0	0.0	6,437.4	70.5	-70.5
Train	359	0.0	0.0	6,437.4	119.6	-119.6
Subway	302	0.0	0.0	3,218.7	50.3	-50.3
Boat	499	0.0	0.0	1,609.3	41.6	-41.6
Airplane	4,246	9,656.1	2,122.8	9,656.1	2,122.8	0.0
Taxi	5,162	0.0	0.0	0.0	0.0	0.0
Tram	646	0.0	0.0	0.0	0.0	0.0
Trolley	574	0.0	0.0	1,609.3	47.9	-47.9
Total Public		9,656.1	2,122.8	28,968.2	2,452.6	-329.8
Private						
Bicycle	104	0.0	0.0	0.0	0.0	0.0
Prius	2,341	0.0	0.0	0.0	0.0	0.0
Honda Fit	3,656	0.0	0.0	0.0	0.0	0.0
Sonata	4,427	19,312.1	4,427.1	0.0	0.0	4,427.1
Caravan	5,561	19,312.1	5,561.1	19,312.1	5,561.1	0.0
Expedition	7,711	0.0	0.0	0.0	0.0	0.0
Yours?	0	0.0	0.0	0.0	0.0	0.0
Total Private		38,624.3	9,988.2	19,312.1	5,561.1	4,427.1
Total All		48,280.3	12,111.0	48,280.3	8,013.7	4,097.3

ᵃ difference

model home for one year! You just won a Bronze Medal. If you are on the Comprehensive Diet Plan and want to calculate your own values, you can download the worksheets at www.climatediet.com/tables.asp. Just fill in your own numbers in the red boxes just like you did with the house zones.

Before we close our discussion of this topic, let's not forget to say something about the most energy-efficient and climate-friendly mode of transportation of all for urban commuters—the trusty bicycle. Contrary to popular belief, human-powered transport is not emissions-free. Like fossil fuel conveyances, we also require energy (in the form of calories) to get from point A to point B. However, riding a bike can be up to 50 times more energy efficient than driving a car. Over 95% of a car's energy use is devoted to moving the car, not the occupant (Stoyke, 2007).

In addition to being more energy efficient, biking provides numerous other benefits to individuals and communities. Like other forms of exercise, bike riding strengthens our body and mind. It generates no particulate emissions. Parking is rarely a problem. Bikes are wonderfully quiet replacements for the noise and polluting conveyances that normally clog modern cities. In fact, many towns and cities are finding that severely limiting or even banning cars altogether has brought new life and vitality to their urban core. Imagine living in a place where people actually smile and wave at one other on their way to work rather than engaging in existential combat for road space in rush hour traffic.

> Riding a bike can be up to 50 times more energy efficient than driving a car.

A Note on Air Transportation

How about air transportation? A raging debate exists on the environmental effects of air travel. If you look at carbon dioxide emissions and distance traveled alone, air travel seems to compare favorably to single occupancy auto travel. However, taxi emissions assume single occupancy. So if you add another passenger, per capita emissions drop by half. There are also a number of other factors to consider. For example, how many takeoffs and landings did you experience during your trip? If you travel on Southwest Airlines in the United States, it is likely you stopped somewhere before reaching your

Table 7.4 Environmental Effects of Air Travel

Round-Trip Flight	Distance miles	Distance km	CO_2/mi	CO_2	CO_2 x 2 (EU adjustment)
Seattle–New York City	4,827	7,767	0.39	1,883	3,766
Vancouver–Toronto	4,155	6,685	0.39	1,620	3,240
San Francisco–Los Angeles	674	1,084	0.39	263	526
Sydney–Perth	4,069	6,547	0.39	1,587	3,174
Auckland–Christchurch	925	1,488	0.39	361	722
New York City–London	6,880	11,070	0.39	2,683	5,366
Los Angeles–Tokyo	10,871	17,491	0.39	4,240	8,480
Chicago–Atlanta	1,211	1,948	0.39	472	944

Source: Flight miles and conversion factor are from www.terrapass.com (2007).

Billions of gallons of jet fuel are wasted every year by planes waiting on tarmacs.

destination. Weather and congestion also have important effects on emissions. Billions of gallons of jet fuel are wasted every year by planes waiting on tarmacs or circling in holding patterns above airports.

Most passenger jets operate at cruising altitudes between 5 and 8 mi (8 to 13 km) above sea level. Consequently, jets deliver GHGs to parts of the atmosphere that are the most vulnerable to their warming effects. Jet propulsion also produces extraordinary amounts of water vapor that form into condensation trails, which, in turn, can develop into cirrus clouds—many scientists believe these clouds also having warming effects. Consequently, the IPCC estimates that the total warming effect of aviation is two to four times higher than from the impact of carbon dioxide alone. European Commission researchers have also concluded that warming effects are about double (European Commission, DG Environment, 2005b).

So if we add these multiplier effects to GHGs generated by jet fuel combustion, our taxi comparison does not look so bad after all. The moral of this story is that you should avoid air travel whenever possible. If you do need to fly, consider offsetting your emissions with carbon credits. Offsetting a 10,800 mi (17,491 km) Los Angeles–Tokyo trip will run you about four metric tons of carbon dioxide.

The Skinny on Ethanol

Now let's briefly discuss some other possible energy alternatives that may or may not help us break our dependence on imported oil and provide cleaner transportation options. During the past few years, ethanol has been embraced by many as the fuel of the future. Farmers in the United States and Europe see ethanol production as a way to revitalize small farm communities and reduce foreign oil dependency. In 2007 U.S. farmers planted more corn than at any time since World War II (Martin, 2007). Riding this wave of interest, Ford and GM now tout "flex fuel" vehicles that can run on ethanol/gas blends such as E-85 (85% ethanol and 15% gasoline).

Most ethanol in North America and Europe is produced from a renewable resource: corn. Also, when burned, it produces about 30% less carbon dioxide emissions than gasoline. Sounds like a sure winner! Well, let's pause and ponder a few potential drawbacks before we jump on the ethanol bandwagon. First, let's examine how much energy it takes to produce ethanol. Corn does not grow on its own. Fields must be tilled and irrigated, harvests must be transported and stored—all of which requires energy. At present, this energy is supplied by fossil fuels. Ethanol-producing plants also require energy. In 2006 plans were in place to build almost 200 new ethanol plants in the United States. Many of the same agricultural cooperatives that store and transport corn are getting into the energy business. These innovative businesses, many of them locally run, are way ahead of their oil industry counterparts in developing this new fuel source. However, there is a problem. Like any business, these cooperatives need to minimize production costs to stay competitive in the marketplace. What do you think is one of the cheapest and most available sources of energy to run these new plants? It is coal, a fossil fuel that the United States still has in abundance. If the ethanol industry adopts coal as its main energy source, the United States may be able to increase its energy independence, but at what cost? The environmental benefits associated with ethanol development would be greatly diminished.

At some distant point in the future, there may be enough ethanol to fuel the whole ethanol production supply chain. But until we reach that point, nonrenewable fossil fuels will still play a key role in ethanol

Ethanol alone will never supply more than a small portion of the world's energy needs.

production. Also, unless we find a new way to produce it, ethanol alone will never supply more than a small portion of the world's energy needs. There is simply not enough farmland available to produce sufficient amounts of the corn or sugarcane needed to replace the millions of barrels per day that we use to keep our economy humming along. Consider, too, that ethanol burns more cleanly than regular gasoline but still generates lots of GHG emissions. And the most popular formation of ethanol-based fuel, E-85, still has a fossil fuel content of 15%, which limits the cost and environmental advantages of this energy source. New technologies may be on the horizon, such as the production of ethanol from cellulose waste, that could change this equation (PR Newswire, 2007).

Other factors also mitigate the benefits of ethanol. The mpg average for E-85 vehicles is significantly lower than gasoline-powered ones. This may drive up the operating costs of E-85 vehicles. Also, at the time of this book's publication, the per-gallon cost of E-85 was higher than gasoline. For example, a 2007 Chevy Impala running on gasoline only gets 21 mpg in the city and 31 mpg on the highway. The same vehicle running on E-85 gets 16 mpg in the city and 23 mpg on the highway. Similarly, running a 2007 Chevy Suburban on E-85 will cut your city mpg from an already paltry 15 mpg to only 11 mpg. Keeping that E-85 Suburban running may cost hundreds more per year than driving its gasoline-powered counterpart (Environmental Protection Agency/Department of Energy, 2007b).

Biodiesel

Another vehicle fuel that is becoming increasingly available in the United States and Europe is biodiesel. Biodiesel can be made from a variety of sources. Typically, alcohol is mixed with fats, oils, or greases from vegetable or animal sources. It is a bit like running your car on a can of supercharged Crisco. Like ethanol, biodiesel has been around for many decades. Some of the first automobiles were run on peanut oil (O'Keefe, 2006).

Biodiesel can be used in almost any car that has a diesel engine. Unfortunately, in some countries, including the United States, small diesel vehicles are almost as scarce at hybrids. This contrasts sharply with the European Union where diesel makes up more than half of all transportation fuel used (European Environment Agency, 2005). After a bout of popularity in the late 1970s and 1980s, diesel autos fell out of fashion with most Americans because earlier-generation diesel engines produced more particulate pollution than their gas counterparts. However, over the years, diesel fuels and combustion systems have become much cleaner. Newer engines now emit less sulfur or GHGs than their gasoline counterparts. Biodiesel is even cleaner. Only 3 lb of carbon dioxide is produced per gallon of biodiesel fuel used, versus 20 lb for regular gasoline.

The main problem with biodiesel is that it is very expensive to make. In 2006 the estimated cost of a new crude oil production plant was $360 per gallon of output capacity versus more than $2,900 per gallon for a biodiesel production plant. However, if oil prices stay above $60–$70 per barrel and economies of scale kick in, this renewable alternative to gasoline will become more price competitive. Presently, biodiesel also shares one important characteristic with ethanol. Most biodiesel (in 2008) is produced using foodstuffs (e.g., soybeans) rather than recycled waste products, which can drive up food prices. Big oil companies have little incentive to invest or encourage the spread of this technology because it competes directly with their own core product: diesel made from crude oil. It does not make much economic sense for these firms to make biodiesel when they produce the same product much more cheaply using existing methods. If ethanol and biodiesel really take off in popularity, this could drive down the value of yet-to-be-tapped oil reserves that oil firms own but have not yet pumped out of the earth.

> Most biodiesel is produced using foodstuffs (e.g., soybeans), which can drive up food prices.

Electric and Hydrogen Power

For more than two decades, environmentalists, engineers, and visionaries have been predicting the imminent arrival of electric- and hydrogen-powered vehicles. On the surface, both fueling technologies seem to offer unbeatable environmental characteristics. Electric cars do not generate any tailpipe emissions when used, while hydrogen cars emit only water. In the late 1990s GM offered the electrically propelled EV-1, which was touted as the next great thing in automotive engineering. It reportedly could accelerate from 0 to 60 in 8.5 seconds and had the lowest drag coefficient ever recorded for a production vehicle. However, this innovative car was unceremoniously withdrawn from the market a few years later. GM's next great electric promise is the Chevy Volt, which is slated for mass production by around 2010. To fill the void, a few small manufacturers are coming out with plug-in kits for existing hybrid vehicles. However, the stock batteries currently sold with these cars are not manufactured to run uninterruptedly for long periods of time. Prius owners who have tried to go this route have found that running their cars on battery power only dramatically reduces battery life. Battery-assisted or independent propulsion systems remain much more costly than conventional combustion engines. Also, those of us who live in colder climes know that battery performance varies considerably along with changes in temperature. In addition, significant hurdles related to battery recycling/disposal must also be overcome.

What about hydrogen power? Actor and California governor Arnold Schwarzenegger received lots of press for converting his Hummer to hydrogen. Some municipalities and large firms throughout the United States maintain small hydrogen-powered auto, bus, or truck fleets. In 2008 BMW, GM, and Daimler plan to roll out hydrogen-powered test fleets of up to 100 vehicles each, certainly not enough to solve the climate crisis. It will be many years before safe (remember the Hindenburg?) and affordable mass-market hydrogen vehicles become available. Even if you could afford to buy one, where would you fill it up? In 2006 there were only 700 miles of hydrogen pipelines versus one million for natural gas in the United States, and only a handful of hydrogen stations (Motavalli, 2007). The U.S. Department of Energy maintains a Web site to help people find filling stations by fuel type. According to a November 2007 search for U.S. hydrogen stations, only 12 states have at least one pump. California led the pack with 37 operating or planned stations, most of which are in and around the San Francisco and Los Angeles metro areas (database can be accessed at www.eere.energy.gov/afdc/fuels/stations_query.html). Only a few of these are open to the general public (I suspect the one on Sacramento, the California state capital, is where Arnold fills up his SUV). Sadly, Washington state has no stations, so I guess it will be some time before

It will be many years before safe and affordable mass-market hydrogen vehicles become available.

Puget Sound residents can jump on the hydrogen bandwagon.

Besides availability and cost, the current main problem with both technologies is that in most cases production of the electricity and hydrogen that propels these new vehicles is still largely derived from fossil fuels. The most cost-efficient method for producing hydrogen is through separation from natural gas (though it is also possible to produce hydrogen using electrolysis, which separates oxygen and water). Globally, most electricity is produced by coal-fired power plants. If your electricity is generated by wind or solar systems, you can largely overcome this problem, but this is rarely the case. Until these challenges are met, electric and hydrogen vehicles will not contribute much to our fight against human-induced climate change. In the near term, we are going to have to learn to make better use of existing technologies and modes of transport to really make a difference.

Conclusion

Transportation emissions are one of the greatest hurdles we face in our war against climate change. Since 1990 transportation emissions have increased in almost every country in the world. In the European Union emissions have been increasing at more than 4% a year. If this growth rate continues, it will offset as much as a quarter of Kyoto Protocol–mandated EU-15 emissions reductions (European Commission, DG Environment, 2005b). Americans are loath to give up their beloved automobiles, and the U.S. government remains resistant to significantly increasing fuel-efficiency standards. However, for most of us, there are plenty of transportation alternatives to driving.

The automobile is not the only culprit, though. One of the main reasons for the fast growth in transportation emissions is transportation market deregulation and the associated rise of discount air carriers. As the price of air travel declines in real terms, more Europeans are taking to the skies. Similar trends are driving demand for air travel in Asia and Oceania. Singapore and Kuala Lumpur have become hubs for deep-discount airlines selling tickets to international destinations for as little as US$19. Air travel expansion in China exceeds the country's 10% annual growth rate.

> In the near term, we are going to have to learn to make better use of existing technologies and modes of transport to really make a difference.

Somehow we have to rein in the temptation to fly. A few long-haul flights can throw the best-planned Climate Diet seriously out of whack. Air travel is especially challenging for business travelers who often have to choose between flying or unemployment. Short of not traveling by air at all, purchasing carbon offsets is the best way to mitigate the climate impact of work- or pleasure-related travel. Road warriors may want to consider encouraging their employers to adopt business models that require less travel or to purchase carbon credits on behalf of employees.

While hurdles lie ahead in our quest for more climate-friendly choices, the potential for making progress remains bright. Never before have so many transportation choices been available. Long-range bus networks, bullet trains, and light rail and subway systems are going up all over the world. And as many cities expand green transportation alternatives, such as bike and walking lanes and trails, many North Americans are waking up to mobility opportunities that Europeans and Asian city dwellers have long embraced—that human power works perfectly well as a way to get from point A to point B.

> Human power works perfectly well as a way to get from point A to point B.

Tips Summary

Model home changes for the transportation zone:

✓   Replace exclusive private vehicle use with a mix of public transportation alternatives.

For additional savings:

✓   Properly maintain private vehicles.

✓   If you need to purchase a vehicle, buy the most fuel-efficient one that will meet your needs.

✓   If you don't drive, you will not burn gas. Decreasing overall auto use is the best way to cut emissions and preserve the useful life of your vehicle. Consider combining small trips or carpooling or using public transportation.

✓ Drive conservatively. Aggressive driving, including hard acceleration and braking, can reduce gas mileage by as much at 33%. Accelerate slowly from a full stop and drive near the speed limit. For every 5 mph over 60 mph (95 km/h), efficiency declines by 10%.

✓ Use the recommended grade of motor oil for your vehicle and keep tires properly inflated—this can improve fuel economy by 5%.

✓ Regularly take your car in for a tune-up and replace air filters when needed. These actions can increase your mileage by an additional 4%.

✓ Avoid letting your vehicle idle. Idling cars get 0 mpg (km/L). If you find yourself sitting in congestion for more than 30 seconds, you will save gas by turning off your engine and then restarting it when traffic starts moving.

✓ Close windows and sunroofs and remove other items that might reduce the aerodynamic characteristics of your vehicle.

✓ Remove extra weight from your vehicle. Each 100 extra pounds can reduce gas mileage by 2%.

✓ Use public transportation, a bicycle, or walk to get around.

✓ Avoid air travel. Consider vacationing closer to home.

Community Strategies for a Better Climate

8

Many of us are chronic dieters. We start with a bang, drop 10 pounds in a month, and then slip back to our old selves—and then some. Why do so many people fall off the wagon when it comes to dieting? One word: community. Dozens of studies have shown that dieting is most successful and long lasting when tackled with a friend. Whole industries have grown up around this premise. It is hard to drive down the road without passing a Weight Watchers or Jenny Craig franchise. Why do people frequent exercise clubs when they could just as easily do their daily jog on a treadmill in the comfort of their own home? Congregating with others engaged in the same fight, whether it is cutting carbon pounds or shedding body fat, motivates us to keep pushing forward. Communities provide advice and support whenever we are tempted to stray from our gold medal–winning ways. In this chapter, we explore a number of strategies for connecting with and building energy-efficient, climate-conscious communities that can solidify our quest for more climate-conscious lifestyles.

> Congregating with others engaged in the same fight . . . motivates us to keep pushing forward.

How Do I Find Fellow Carbon Cutters?

Luckily, you shouldn't have too much trouble finding fellow carbon-cutting warriors. There is no shortage of groups that have jumped on the climate-change bandwagon. Table 8.1 provides a list of U.S. and international environmental organizations you might want to investigate. Seek out an entity with an active local chapter that provides opportunities to really get down and dirty: to restore rivers, streams, and other habitats threatened by global warming.

If you do not like any of the environmentally oriented groups in your area, think about starting your own. For instance, faith-based organizations are a natural place to start, as a strong community is often already in place. If you are a church member, consider asking your fellow parishioners if they might be interested in starting a climate-change discussion group. This is already happening in thousands of religious organizations. In October 2006 more than 4,000 churches in the United States hosted free showings of Al Gore's *An Inconvenient Truth* (Gore, West, and Guggenheim, 2006). Hundreds of congregations seized on this opportunity to start environmental Bible studies. Many church members have also taken pledges to cut their household emissions.

> Faith-based organizations are a natural place to start.

Table 8.1 **List of Major Environmental Organizations**

Organization	Membership
Sierra Club (U.S.)	550,000
Audubon Society (U.S.)	600,000
National Wildlife Federation (U.S.)	440,000
The Nature Conservancy (U.S.)	1,000,000
World Wildlife Fund (U.S.)	1,200,000
Environmental Defense Fund (U.S.)	500,000
Greenpeace (worldwide)	2,800,000
Natural Resource Defense Council (U.S.)	1,200,000
Friends of the Earth (UK)	1,000,000

Note: Membership numbers from early 2000s.

Source: Vig and Kraft (2003) and organizational Web sites.

How High Wind Made a Difference: One Person at a Time

Individuals and communities can make a real difference. One case in point is my own aunt and uncle's successful effort to promote new ways of thinking about "walking more gently on the Earth." In the middle of the oil shocks and stagflation of the 1970s, they founded an "intentional community" on their own farm. The residents of High Wind, Wisconsin, adopted a grand strategy to prove to the world that it was possible to greatly reduce their use of fossil fuels. They built new structures that incorporated state-of-the-art energy and conservation technologies. Attics and windows were superinsulated. New houses were constructed to maximize their exposure to southern sunlight. On clear days, larger masonry walls, floors, and hearthstones were bathed in sunlight. Then at night energy radiated from these structures, decreasing the need for heating fuel. Each house also used superefficient wood-burning stoves rather than natural gas to keep interior temperatures comfortable during the long winter months.

The community also worked to become food self-sufficient. Decades before the natural and organic foods retailer Whole Foods entered the scene, their land was turned over to intensive organic farming. Low- or no-till cultivation techniques preserved the quality of the soil and drastically reduced methane, nitrous oxide, and carbon emissions. Community members religiously reused and recycled everything. They even took a crack at raising fish.

We can learn a number of lessons from High Wind and other similar communities. First, if they were able to make drastic cuts in their fossil fuel use in the 1970s and 1980s, why can't we do it today? The formerly cutting-edge technologies they used then are now widely available. They are also far cheaper. For instance, the current per-watt cost of solar electrical generation is 90% lower than it was in the 1970s (*The Economist*, 2007). How much more do you think it costs to orient houses to maximize sun exposure? Nothing!

Some people still believe that only rich people can afford cutting-edge energy-efficient technologies (I hope by now you have been convinced otherwise). I recently asked my uncle Bel about this issue. He stated that the overall construction cost of his High Wind home was no higher per square foot than similarly sized conventional structures. Furthermore, he estimates that his family has saved tens of thousands of dollars and more than 300 tons of GHG emissions over the years. He and his wife did have to commute to the city a few days a week for work or shopping. However, they chose to reorganize their work and social lives so they could work and play close to home. They have driven the most fuel-efficient automobiles available. In the 1990s they owned a Honda Civic VX getting around 50 mpg on the highway. Now they own a Prius.

Yes, going on a Climate Diet is not only within the reach of rich yuppies. Everyone can do it. It can save you money. But more importantly, it is the right thing to do. The founders of High Wind were not just a bunch of technology geeks. Their motivations were far more profound. First and foremost, they were on a moral crusade, a mission to save the planet from environmental destruction, and to show the world that there are real, viable alternatives to the fossil fuel–driven, throwaway culture of developed nations. High Winders came from various spiritual (or nonspiritual) backgrounds and walks of life: Christians, Jews, Buddhists, Hindus, and Animists all lived in the same community. They were united by a common bond—their love for the planet and the overriding need to take concrete action to protect it. They had a holistic understanding of the human species and its relationship with the natural world. This environmental ethic was not only naturally sound, but it also informed an overall morality that embraced a love of life in all its forms. They understood that humans were quickly exceeding the carrying capacity of the wonderfully intricate but fragile spaceship we call Earth and that we must protect what we have. It is our only option (High Wind, 2007).

Building More Environmentally Friendly Communities

The High Wind example illustrates that how we live and how our communities function are just as important as the products we buy or the energy we use. The fact of the matter is, we need to apply lessons learned from small enclaves like High Wind on a massive scale. Cities are often seen as enemies of the environment. However, if they are planned right, they can be allies in our fight against climate change. We can do many things to encourage the development of more efficient, environmentally aware, and better-planned metropolitan communities.

> We need to apply lessons learned from small enclaves like High Wind on a massive scale.

Western Washington State is a region that is often held up as a paragon of environmental virtue. Local residents love to brag about their Earth-friendly values. However, their driving and living habits tell a different story. As in other parts of the country, Washingtonians love their cars. The four-county Seattle-Tacoma-Everett metropolitan area is home to more than three million people. Most of the communities in this area are served by public transit. Table 8.2 provides statistics on comparative driving habits among Northwest inhabitants. In 2004 Washington state residents used 8.1 gal of gasoline (30.7 L) per capita per week. This is an improvement over 1990, when the number was 8.7 gal (32.9 L). This trend also compares favorably to the rest of the country, where per capita gasoline use increased 0.4 gal (1.5 L) over the same period. However, Washington's per capita gasoline use is only average in relation to neighboring states. Also, it is substantially higher than Canada's closest province, British Columbia (Northwest Environment Watch [now called Sightline Institute], 2006).

Table 8.2 Weekly Per Capita Gasoline and Diesel Use in the Northwest: 1990 and 2004

Location	Gas Use PC		Hwy Diesel Use PC	
	1990	2004	1990	2004
Washington	8.7 (32.9 L)	8.1 (30.7 L)	1.4 (5.3 L)	2.0 (7.6 L)
Northwest States	8.8 (31.3 L)	8.1 (30.7 L)	1.8 (6.8 L)	2.3 (8.7 L)
British Columbia	5.1 (19.3 L)	5.3 (20.1 L)	1.2 (4.5 L)	1.7 (6.4 L)
Canada	5.6 (21.2 L)	5.8 (22.0 L)	1.1 (4.2 L)	1.7 (6.4 L)
United States	8.4 (31.8 L)	8.8 (31.3 L)	1.6 (6.1 L)	2.4 (9.1 L)

Note: Values denote weekly use and are in gallons. One gal = 3.785 L.

Source: Sightline Institute (2006).

Table 8.3 Urban Sprawl in Selected Cities: 1990 and 2000

Location	Population		Growth	% Compact	
	1990	2000	1990-2000(%)	1990	2000
Boise (Ada County)	206,000	301,000	46	3	7
Victoria BC (Capital Regional District)	281,000	314,000	12	33	34
Spokane (Spokane County)	361,000	418,000	16	8	10
Eugene (Lane County)	283,000	323,000	14	10	12
Portland (3 Oregon counties)	1,175,000	1,445,000	23	23	28
Seattle (3 counties)	2,562,000	3,045,000	19	21	24
Vancouver BC (Greater Victoria Regional District)	1,600,000	2,013,000	26	51	62

Note: "Compact" refers to the percentage of residents who live in compact communities.

Source: Northwest Environment Watch (now called Sightline Institute), 2004.

What gives? British Columbia is much larger than Washington. The province's wide-open spaces rival those of any American state, with the possible exception of Alaska. Most British Columbia residents drive the same types of automobiles. The climate is similar. Given these circumstances, you would think that British Columbia residents should use more rather than less gasoline.

Decades ago, British Columbia citizens and their elected officials made a conscious decision to follow in the footsteps of their European brethren. Yes, they could have copied the U.S. model of suburbia, but they chose a different direction by building more compact communities (12 or more people per square acre). Table 8.3 shows the results of this trend. By 2000 more than 60% of Vancouver metro residents lived in compact communities versus only about one-quarter of Seattle metro residents. Even the relatively rural island community of Victoria does better.

Population Growth and the Atmosphere

All communities must confront the challenge of population growth.

All communities must confront the challenge of population growth, which, in the aggregate, often has negative environmental consequences. The average American child will emit 13 times more GHGs than the average Bangladeshi during a lifetime (WRI, 2006). In Lester Brown's (1995) *Who Will Feed China?* he discusses how the combination of a growing Chinese population and consumption rates put the planet's future food supply and overall environmental security at risk.

Is population growth a primary driver behind our current climate crisis? The answer is yes . . . *but*. The source of the problem is not just the sheer number of people living on this planet, but *how* they live their lives. China and other less-wealthy countries are adopting the same unsustainable growth model that developed nations popularized, such as encouraging ownership of private automobiles and increasingly more energy-intensive lifestyles. As a student of Chinese history, language, and culture, I have been traveling to China for more than three decades. During my first trip to Guangzhou in 1978, I was struck by how few motorized vehicles were in the streets. The bellowing of occasional automobiles was drowned out by the ringing bells of bicyclists jockeying for position. In fact, more street space was reserved for bicycles than for trucks and autos. Fast-forward 10 years. Automobiles and motorcycles ruled the road; bicycle lanes were still around, but had shrunk considerably. And now? Well, have you ever been to lower Manhattan during rush hour? You get the picture.

The moral of this story is that how you choose to live is at least as important as how many children you have. Family size is an intensely personal decision. It is very difficult to balance the potential environmental costs of having more children with the potential social benefits. Strict population control is not a cure-all for global warming. What we need to do is think about how we can minimize our household impact on the planet. I have many friends and relatives who have large families but are also models of efficiency. My cousin Ted and his wife, Bunny, have six grown children. During the early days when everyone was living under one roof, I was amazed at how organized their home was. Rather than buying a mansion, Ted and Bunny chose to make do with an average-size house. Everyone shared a bedroom. Bunny bought in bulk long before big box discount supermarkets ever existed. During dinnertime, their kitchen resembled an army mess hall with everyone pitching in. Nothing went to waste. When family members outgrew clothes or toys, they passed them on to someone else. Ted was always busy fixing vehicles and appliances around the house, keeping them in good shape rather than trading them in for new models. Now each of their children has a large family. But the children have not forgotten the conservationist values they were raised with and are passing them on to the next generation.

How you choose to live is at least as important as how many children you have.

Environmentally Friendly Investment

Another way to encourage climate-friendly communities is to invest in cutting-edge industries and causes while avoiding organizations that do not share your values. In recent years "socially responsible" mutual funds and other investment vehicles have proliferated. This is one avenue for putting your money to work for the climate. Socially responsible investments are not only good for the environment, but also for your pocketbook. Morningstar (2006), the big mutual funds rating firm, noted that between 2001 and 2006 socially responsible funds outperformed the S&P 500, one of the world's major stock indexes.

Invest in cutting-edge industries and causes.

Why? Because most of these socially responsible funds are directing money into growing new sectors of the economy, such as biofuel production, solar power, and superefficient heating, cooling, and power-generation technologies (Odell, 2007).

When evaluating how to invest your money responsibly, avoid firms that refuse to openly disclose or quantify the financial risks associated with ignoring global warming. The global insurance industry was an early convert to the need to assess global warming risk. Swiss Re, one of the largest insurance firms in the world, estimated that the direct costs of global warming–related events (flooding, desertification, spread of contagious diseases, severe weather, etc.) in 2004 was over US$30 billion (Heck, Bresch, and Trober, 2006). Dozens of public pension funds now demand that firms they invest in assess and report climate-change risk to investors (Ceres, 2006). Many of these funds also expect corporations to meet stringent codes of ethical conduct, including environmental responsibility, as a precondition for investment consideration. Some of the largest carbon dioxide emitters in the United States, including large electric-generation public utilities, have responded to calls from investors to develop concrete action plans to reduce GHG emissions (Sierra Club, 2005). One of the most prominent of these efforts, the Pew Climate Coalition, has enlisted dozens of corporations in its GHG-reduction action initiative (Pew Trust, 2006).

According to the Carbon Disclosure Project (2007), which was established by large institutional investors to assess trends in risks and opportunities associated with climate change and its mitigation, some old industrial standard bearers are taking notice of new investment and consumption trends. In 2007 the project sent out questionnaires to all *Financial Times* Global 500 companies regarding their climate impact. Seventy-seven percent of companies voluntarily provided an accounting of their GHG emissions. The survey revealed that large firms that view climate change mitigation as a business opportunity rather than a burden, including multinationals such as Dupont and General Electric (GE), are pouring billions of dollars into developing more efficient products and services, which are among the fastest growing segments of their businesses.

Once an environmental laggard, Dupont is now recognized as a leader in the corporate fight to reduce emissions. In the late 1980s, the company voluntarily agreed to phase out production of ozone-depleting chlorofluorocarbons (CFCs). It is now working to phase out hydrofluorocarbons (HFCs). It has made a commitment to reduce GHG emissions 65% below 1990 levels by 2010 by phasing out GHG-emitting products, higher capacity utilization, process changes, and increased use of alternative energy. Dupont also estimates that its GHG-reduction strategy since 1990 has saved more than $2 billion on energy costs alone (Pew Trust, 2006).

GE has also turned the need for emissions reduction into a new business opportunity. The firm has established a companywide goal to increase energy efficiency and reduce waste in all market segments. GE's Eco-imagination campaign touts the environmental credentials of everything from Energy Star dishwashers to jet engines. GE's new engines are standard equipment on Boeing's new 787 Dreamliner passenger jet, which uses 20% less fuel than comparable planes (Pfiefer, 2007).

Even foreign oil firms like BP and Royal Dutch Shell are investing hundreds of millions of dollars into alternative energy and GHG-mitigation technologies like carbon sequestration, in which carbon dioxide is pumped into deep geologic formations for future storage. Admittedly, most of their investment dollars still go to their core business—fossil fuel production. However, they are well ahead of many U.S. firms in taking steps to develop alternative energy technologies (Ceres, 2006).

In short, investing in future technologies creates new jobs, increases the competitiveness of firms, and improves shareholder investment returns, all of which can mean more money for you and your family.

Carbon Offsets

We said in earlier chapters that you can purchase carbon offsets as a proxy for decreasing your family's carbon emissions. New financial instruments allow investors to easily buy and sell carbon just like other commodities. For example, if my family wants to offset the carbon dioxide emitted by our automobile, we can pay an offsetting firm like TerraPass or Native Energy, to either buy emissions offsets from a carbon exchange or invest our contribution in a carbon emissions–mitigating activity (e.g., building wind farms). Since carbon dioxide emissions are not heavily regulated in the United States or large developing countries like China and India, these investments are mostly voluntary. However, more and more individuals, businesses, and government entities are choosing to offset their carbon dioxide emissions anyway. In fact, so many entities are buying and selling their right to pollute that a new U.S.-based commodities exchange, the Chicago Climate Exchange, was created to facilitate these transactions.

It should be noted that not all carbon offsets are created equal. For instance, the science behind the benefits of creating carbon sinks by planting trees is fuzzy at best. Estimates of the amount of carbon sequestered by forests vary widely. Also, trees do not permanently offset GHGs. When they die (or go up in flames) they release carbon dioxide back into the atmosphere. Also, you need to determine whether creating a new forest or other carbon sink is really providing a net additional benefit that would not otherwise occur without human intervention. The offsetting benefits of replacing coal-produced electricity with wind- or solar-generated power is much less ambiguous. Also, we should choose offsetting programs that are actively expanding their renewable energy investments rather than just resting on their laurels.

The idea of buying and selling pollution rights is not new. In the 1980s another environmental threat—acid rain—endangered the viability of the forests of the northeast United States and eastern Canada. Acid rain is mainly caused by excessive sulfur dioxide emissions—electric utilities that maintained coal-burning power plants were the primary source of emissions. This powerful gas floated into the atmosphere, mixing with other chemicals during its journey, and finally fell back to earth as a powerful acid during rainstorms. To control this threat, the U.S. government, Canada, regional state governments, and private industry created a mandatory regime that would control the growth of sulfur dioxide emissions. Sulfur emitters were required to pay for the right to pollute, and emissions caps were set for all large polluters. Furthermore, a sliding scale was created that decreased allowable emissions each year. Companies that could not meet the new yearly requirements had three choices: They could choose to carry on business as usual by purchasing the right to create more pollution from firms that were below their caps. Second, they could install new

More and more individuals, businesses, and government entities are choosing to offset their carbon dioxide emissions.

equipment that would decrease their emissions to allowable levels. Or third, they could scale back or shut down heavily polluting operations. This system established clear and quantifiable consequences for polluting. The philosophy was simple—if you pollute, you pay.

The United States was an innovator in this cap-and-trade market, which shares many similarities with the European Union Greenhouse Gas Emissions Trading Scheme (EU-ETS) now being implemented by the European Union as part of its Kyoto Protocol commitment. The main reason why this system worked for the acid rain problem in the 1980s is because it took obvious existing social and environmental costs associated with energy production and encouraged electricity producers to internalize these costs in their own price structures. Before the policy was established, polluters got off scot-free for the damage they were doing to the environment, while the rest of us watched forests die, watersheds decline, and fish stocks deteriorate. Isn't it fair to ask polluters to pay for the damage they inflict, rather than expecting society to bear the entire cost? This is what cap and trade is all about. It worked for sulfur dioxide. It can also work to cut GHG emissions. But if the biggest GHG emitter, the United States, does not join the regime, cap and trade will never achieve its full potential as a market-based approach to combating global warming (Bayon, 2002).

> Isn't it fair to ask polluters to pay for the damage they inflict, rather than expecting society to bear the entire cost?

Voting and Political Activism

If we do not let our elected officials know that we care about global warming, they will not do something about it until it is too late. Politicians have one overriding goal—re-election. Few will actually admit this fact. However, their actions tell us otherwise. How much time do you think the average freshman congressman or member of Parliament spends writing legislation or formulating policy? How much time do you think these representatives of the people spend on claiming credit (lecturing constituents about all the great things they have done for their district) and fund-raising?

Voters need to make it clear to elected officials that they care about climate change. The first thing we need to do is educate ourselves about the candidates. How climate friendly are their voting records?

> Voters need to make it clear to elected officials that they care about climate change.

In the United States, the League of Conservation Voters keeps track of the voting records of national and state elected representatives. Friends of the Earth serves a similar role in the United Kingdom. National branches of Greenpeace and the World Wildlife Fund keep an eye on elections across much of the European Union. Check out their Web sites and educate yourself.

The second step is to let your elected representatives know what you think. Tell them that their environmental stance is an important factor in your voting decision. Join letter campaign drives to save endangered species or attend a political rally. If enough people stand up to do this, it may have an effect. Third, actively work to get climate-friendly politicians elected. Every candidate needs extra volunteers. Man the telephones, distribute flyers, go door to door, or speak publicly about your favorite candidates' climate change positions.

I understand that many voters out there face a dilemma. Yes, they would like to vote for a climate-friendly politician. But many pro-environment candidates may be members of the "wrong" party. This is especially true in the United States where if you are a conservative Republican, it is likely the pro-environment candidate is on the wrong side of other burning issues that you may care about, such as abortion, gay marriage, or school prayer. These are all important moral issues. However, I hope that after reading this book you will also agree that global warming is an important moral issue as well. The consequences of human-induced climate change are already bringing great suffering to humanity. And evidence is growing every day that things will get much worse in the near future. Many of its victims are our own children who are too young to make choices about how they live. Why put their futures at risk? Yes, we can make a difference by making voluntary changes in the way we live. Yet, if government and social institutions do not follow our lead, it will be more difficult to turn the corner on this great threat to our children's future.

Our choices as consumers, investors, voters, and community organizers and activists all have the potential to transform our relationship with the climate. Reducing commutes and building vibrant communities that are not dependent on private vehicle transportation diminish our climate disrupting footprints and improve our quality of life. If enough consumers choose to live in compact communities, buy carbon offsets, make environmentally responsible investments, take public transportation, live conservationist lifestyles, and vote responsibly, big business and government will follow. As they are not yet fully committed to building a carbon-neutral world, we need to take the lead to build a better future for our children.

Tips Summary

✓ Join an environmental group, or start your own.

✓ Buy carbon offsets.

✓ Buy green power.

✓ Invest in environmentally responsible companies.

✓ Give careful thought to how you can manage the GHG effects of having a larger family.

✓ Vote for climate-friendly politicians.

✓ Be willing to speak out and educate people about climate change.

✓ Move to a compact community.

Putting It All Together: *Your* Climate Diet Results

9

How Did You Do? Carbon Dioxide Emissions

In the preceding chapters, we discussed a myriad of easy strategies that can be used to reduce our carbon footprint. Chapter 2 described ten good reasons to go on a Climate Diet. Chapter 3 covered the basic methodology used in the Climate Diet. Chapters 4 and 5 presented dozens of cost-effective methods that reduced our carbon "weight" by more than 18,000 lb (8,354 kg) and cut our energy costs by more than $1,600. In chapter 6, we learned more about how the wonderful world of shopping and eating affects our atmosphere and that making better food choices and cutting down on household waste can cut our GHG emissions. Chapter 7 chronicled the high cost of private vehicle use and discussed transportation alternatives that can help us shed an additional 9,033 lb (4,101 kg) of carbon dioxide. Finally, chapter 8 expounded on the virtues of dieting with a friend, building fewer unsustainable communities, supporting environmentally oriented businesses and organizations, and using the ballot box to create more climate-friendly political institutions.

Now comes the moment you have been waiting for. How did you do? How much carbon weight did you lose? Table 9.1 summarizes the climate effects of suggested lifestyle changes to our model household. It also provides an opportunity for you to total up your own calculations if you have them. First, let's find out your total household reduction. A few simple and easy lifestyle changes reduced overall emissions by about 40% or 32,000 lb (14,528 kg).

How much carbon weight did you lose?

We earned a Bronze Medal or better in every household zone. I guess we should go back and work on that "tire" around our waistline a bit more. Making the transition from a two-car to a one-car lifestyle brought the biggest gains among all categories. It looks like it is time to trade in our car keys for a bus or subway pass. Finally, changes in eating and waste disposal habits reduced emissions by more than 5,100 lb (2,315 kg).

Overall, here is our medal tally:

Bronze Medal: six, plus another bronze for overall reductions
Silver Medal: six

This is not a bad haul, don't you think?

Table 9.1 **How Did You Do? CO_2 Emissions**

Zone	Current—Where You Are			Future—Where You Want to Be			CO_2 Cut
	CO_2/yr (lb)	CO_2/yr (kg)	% total CO_2	CO_2/yr (lb)	CO_2/yr (kg)	% Total CO_2	
Household areas							
Living/Dining	3,787.99	1,718.20	5%	2,094.40	950.01	4%	45%
Kitchen	6,312.23	2,863.18	8%	4,607.17	2,089.78	9%	27%
Bedroom 1/Kid's Room	578.88	262.58	1%	256.91	116.53	1%	56%
Bedroom 2/ Master Suite	2,260.56	1,025.37	3%	801.65	363.62	2%	65%
Bedroom 3/ Home Office	1,285.68	583.2	2%	504.70	228.93	1%	61%
Bathrooms	1,076.79	488.63	1%	345.77	156.84	1%	68%
Laundry/Utility	9,036.80	4,107.54	11%	6,158.17	2,795.75	13%	32%
Heating (gas)	12,322.40	5,589.35	15%	5,146.21	2,334.28	11%	58%
Cooling	2,048.72	929.28	3%	1,671.52	758.19	3%	18%
Yard	1,192.51	540.91	1%	420.86	190.90	1%	65%
Shopping							
Food	6,210.16	2,822.80	8%	4,468.64	2,031.20	9%	28%
Waste	7,759.90	3,519.83	10%	4,385.48	1,989.22	9%	43%
Transport	26,700.00	12,111.00	33%	17,667.00	8,013.67	36%	34%
Other Zone	——	——	——	——	——	——	——
Grand Totals	80,572.61	36,561.87	100%	48,528.47	22,018.91	100%	40%

Note: All table values are calculated using Microsoft Excel and are rounded to five decimal places, so grand totals in lb or kg may slightly differ.

How Did You Do? Cost

How much money did our model household save? Table 9.2 only includes changes in household energy costs, which dropped by more than $1,600. Savings would be much more substantial in Europe, Australia, or Japan where energy prices are higher. Check out Appendix C for average energy tariffs in your country. Costs in other zones vary too much from country to country to provide meaningful comparisons. However, it is safe to say that buying less stuff and cutting one private vehicle from your life will save you lots of additional money.

As mentioned throughout this book, you can download all the tables used in the Climate Diet from www.climatediet.com/tables. The tables are set up to automatically tally your total for each diet zone. You can use the default values or enter your own.

You can download all the tables used in the Climate Diet from www. climatediet.com/ tables.asp.

Table 9.2 **How Did You Do? Cost**

Zone	Current—Where You Are		Future—Where You Want to Be			
	Old kWh	Old Cost Total	New kWh	New Cost Total	$ Cost Reduction	% Cost Reduction
Household Zones						
Living/Dining	2,779.15	295.98	1,536.61	163.65	132.33	44.71%
Kitchen	4,631.13	493.22	3,380.17	359.99	133.23	27.01%
Bedroom 1/ Kid's Room	424.71	45.23	188.49	20.07	25.16	55.62%
Bedroom 2/ Master Suite	1,658.46	176.63	588.26	62.65	113.98	64.53%
Bedroom 3/ Home Office	943.27	100.46	370.28	39.44	61.02	60.74%
Bathrooms	790.01	84.14	253.69	27.02	57.12	67.89%
Laundry/Utility	6,630.10	706.11	4,518.10	481.18	224.93	31.85%
Heating		1,329.30		555.16	774.14	58.24%
Cooling	1,503.09	160.08	1,226.36	130.61	29.47	18.41%
Yard	874.94	93.18	308.79	32.89	60.29	64.71%
Grand Totals		3,484.31		1,872.64	1,611.67	46.26%

Summary of Climate Diet Recommendations

The following is a summary of suggested changes made to our model home:

Household Zones

✓ Switch incandescent lighting to CFL equivalent in all zones.

✓ Install one new ceiling fan (bedroom 1).

✓ Replace space heater with an electric blanket (bedroom 2).

✓ Purchase a new Energy Star 19-inch LCD monitor (bedroom 3).

✓ Purchase a new Energy Star printer (bedroom 3).

✓ Cease using home copier (bedroom 3).

✓ Install solar tube lighting fixtures (living/dining).

✓ Cease using two small appliances (kitchen).

✓ Cease using dishwasher (kitchen).

✓ Cease using hair dryers (bathrooms).

✓ Purchase a front-loading washing machine (laundry/utility).

✓ Reduce bathroom water use by taking shorter showers (laundry/utility).

✓ Wrap water heaters and leading piping in insulation to minimize heat loss (laundry/utility).

✓ Reduce hot water heater setting from 140° F (60° C) to 104° F (40° C) (laundry/utility).

✓ Consider forgoing use of hot water for clothes washing (laundry/utility).

✓ Air dry washed clothes whenever possible (laundry/utility).

✓ Weatherize living area (heating and cooling).

✓ Replace a 78% efficient gas furnace with a 90% efficient one (heating).

✓ Replace two conventional room air conditioners with Energy Star 10,000 Btu room air conditioners (cooling).

✓ Cease using leaf blower (yard).

✓ Create a climate-appropriate wildlife habitat that reduces use of yard equipment by half (yard).

Shopping Zone

✓ Reduce consumption of meat and increase consumption of vegetables.

✓ Increase recycling rate to 60% and reduce total garbage volume by 25%.

Transportation Zone

✓ Replace private vehicle use with a mix of public transportation alternatives.

✓ Cut back on air travel.

Here is a list of other carbon dieting tips discussed in *The Climate Diet* that are not included in our model household calculations:

✓ Try living in a smaller home.

✓ Use room fans to more evenly distribute conditioned air.

✓ Cut back on watching TV, which saves time and energy for more important things in life.

✓ Always purchase high-efficiency office equipment if needed.

✓ Be aware of the potential climate impact of nonhuman companions.

✓ Design living/dining room areas to maximize sunlight.

✓ Create living/dining room lighting zones that allow you to maintain high illumination in actively used areas while reducing illumination in unused areas.

✓ Solicit LEED-qualified contractors for remodeling/construction jobs.

✓ Consider installing natural gas piping in kitchen/utility areas to allow use of natural gas appliances.

✓ Use high-efficiency cooking pots/kettles to maximize heat transfer and minimize heat loss during cooking.

✓ Rid your life of unnecessary small appliances.

✓ Conduct an energy audit and carry out necessary weatherizing activities.

✓ Reduce winter interior temperature by 4° F and increase summer temperature by 4° F, which will cut your emissions by as much as 3,500 lb (1,589 kg).

✓ Properly maintain heating and cooling systems and repair ductwork when necessary.

✓ Install and prominently display a "smart meter," which allows you to accurately monitor energy use.

✓ Avoid use of power yard tools, especially gas-powered ones, whenever possible. Try using a human-powered push reel mower for lawn maintenance.

✓ Avoid using outdoor patio heaters.

✓ Develop a local-climate-appropriate low-maintenance yard with natural habitats for nonhuman residents.

✓ Avoid overly packaged food products.

✓ Consider reducing or eliminating consumption of meat, especially red meat.

✓ Increase vegetable consumption.

✓ Buy locally produced organic products.

✓ Avoid nonseasonal foods that require significant shipping methods (e.g., Chilean grapes in winter).

✓ Frequent farmers' markets.

✓ Compost more often.

✓ Avoid animal husbandry items raised under inhumane rearing practices.

✓ Use products made from sustainably harvested or recycled materials.

✓ Give nonmaterial gifts.

✓ Just buy less stuff. Spend less time shopping.

✓ Leave your recreational off-road vehicles at home.

✓ Properly maintain private vehicles.

✓ If you need to purchase a vehicle, buy the most fuel-efficient one that will meet your needs.

✓ If you don't drive, you will not burn gas. Decreasing overall auto use is the best way to cut emissions and preserve the useful life of your vehicle. Consider combining small trips or carpooling or using public transportation.

✓ Drive conservatively. Aggressive driving, including hard acceleration and braking, can reduce gas mileage by as much at 33%. Accelerate slowly from a full stop and drive near the speed limit. For every 5 mph over 60 mph (95 km/h), efficiency declines by 10%.

✓ Use the recommended grade of motor oil for your vehicle and keep tires properly inflated—this can improve fuel economy by 5%.

✓ Regularly take your car in for a tune-up and replace air filters when needed. These actions can increase your mileage by an additional 4%.

✓ Avoid idling your vehicle. Idling cars get 0 mpg (km/L). If you find yourself sitting in congestion for more than 30 seconds, you will save gas by turning off and then restarting your engine when traffic starts moving.

✓ Close windows and sunroofs and remove other items that might reduce the aerodynamic characteristics of your vehicle.

✓ Remove extra weight from your vehicle. Each 100 extra pounds can reduce gas mileage by 2%.

✓ Use public transportation, walk, or ride a bicycle to get around.

✓ Avoid air travel. Consider vacationing closer to home.

✓ Join an environmental group or start your own.

✓ Buy carbon offsets.

✓ Buy green power.

✓ Invest in environmentally responsible companies.

Vote for climate-friendly politicians.

   Move to a compact community.

Other Climate Diet Tips: Carbon-Neutral and Renewable Power Options

We can adopt numerous additional strategies beyond what has already been discussed in *The Climate Diet* to achieve even more emissions savings. The mother lode of sustainable development is cheap renewable energy. We can jump on the renewable energy bandwagon in three ways. First, we can either directly purchase or invest in renewable energy projects (e.g., by purchasing certified carbon offsets). Second, we can purchase renewable energy from a utility or other producer. Hundreds of public and private utilities now offer consumers the option to purchase green power. For instance, in the Seattle area green power can be had for as little as 10% to 15% more per kWh than regular electricity. Some utilities in the United Kingdom sell renewable energy at the same price charged for conventional sources.

Third, we can use passive and active technologies that allow us to produce our own energy. This may include building a home to maximize sunlight, installing high-efficiency windows, or purchasing solar panels. Dozens of books have been written on this topic. One of my favorites is *Smart Power: An Urban Guide to Renewable Energy and Efficiency* by William Kemp (2004). It has never been easier or more cost effective to outfit our homes with solar energy panels, passive solar water heaters, or windmills. As energy prices continue their endless upward march, home energy production and cost savings from household systems will multiply. Most jurisdictions provide subsidies to home owners who want to get into the energy production business. You may even be able to sell your excess energy to your local utility for a profit.

Woodstove heating might be a good choice for some households. Wood heaters have become much more efficient over the years. To get the most out of wood use, you need access to a cheap and sustainably produced source of wood, and a high-efficiency wood stove (conventional fireplaces will not do). The primary downside of wood burning is particulate emissions. Therefore, wood burning is mainly an option for relatively rural communities.

If you purchase enough green power or carbon offsets or supply your own energy needs by investing in a household passive/active or wind-power system, you can technically cancel out all your emissions (assuming that all offsetting activities are as effective as they are advertised to be, which is problematic to determine). In other words, you can become carbon neutral. However, there is no substitute for making lifestyle changes. Altering the way we connect to one another and the environment can have a truly transformative effect on how we view the world around us and can strengthen our awareness of the natural world and fortify our relationships with our family, friends, and communities. Conservation can cure the dreaded disease of affluenza that grips modern life. No amount of carbon credit purchases can accomplish these goals.

Conservation can cure the dreaded disease of affluenza that grips modern life.

Epilogue:
Our Lifestyle—
Her Life

.10

The Climate Diet: Summary Steps

This book has provided a lengthy list of easy, economical strategies we can take that will immediately cut our energy consumption. Let's summarize the Climate Diet one more time. You can go on a Climate Diet in three ways: (1) the Shortest-Cut Diet Plan, (2) the Shortcut Diet Plan, or (3) the Full Home Audit and Comprehensive Diet Plan. All three of these Gold Medal plans include six steps:

1. Get the facts: Learn about the causes of and solutions to the global warming threat.

2. Make a decision: Choose to make a difference by starting along the path toward living a more sustainable and healthier lifestyle.

3. Set goals: Remember that you can tailor your level of participation in ways that will fit your lifestyle. Plan to change a few lightbulbs (Participant), match Kyoto Protocol cuts in GHG emissions (Bronze), or go for the Gold (75% reduction in GHG emissions). Every little bit helps.

4. Count your (carbon) calories: Use your newfound knowledge to make real, quantifiable cuts in your carbon footprint.

5. Get involved: Dieting is usually more effective (and fun) if you do it with a friend. Help your family and community adopt more climate-conscious lifestyles.

6. Evaluate and monitor: Did you achieve your planned dieting milestones?

Chapter 9, "Putting It All Together: *Your* Climate Diet Results," provides a framework for determining how you did. It allows you to evaluate your strengths and weaknesses and summarizes suggestions made throughout the book that you can use to maintain and improve your *Climate Diet* outcomes.

The Climate Diet:
A New Lifestyle for a New Century

For centuries, Europeans, Japanese, North Americans, and the citizens of other economically developed nations have enjoyed Mother Earth's wonderful bounty, which has brought great riches and higher living standards. But it has come at a steep price. Our insatiable desire for Wal-Mart shopping, energy-intensive lifestyles, and unbridled economic growth has greatly exceeded the carrying capacity of our world. Our unsustainable use of the Earth's resources, stolen from our children, is bringing environmental catastrophe to the globe.

Stephen Hawking, one of the preeminent scientists of the 20th century, believes that global warming is one of the greatest threats humankind faces. At a 2006 scientific conference in Beijing, Hawking not so flippantly referred to global warming, noting that Earth "might end up like Venus at 250° C (482° F) and raining sulfuric acid" (Olesen, 2006). Recent probes reveal that Venus's own greenhouse effect, driven by miles-high clouds of carbon dioxide and methane gases trap the sun's heat, creating a fiery furnace uninhabitable to any known form of life. While few people predict this will occur any time soon on Earth, it is not beyond the realm of possibility that it could happen over tens or hundreds of thousands of years, wiping all life from the face of our own planet.

We now face a new destiny. We cannot wait for politicians or captains of industry to discover the issue of global warming. As moral decision makers, we can act to change this state of affairs. We all have it within our power to modify the way we live in ways that are more sustainable. Cutting our use of fossil fuels has never been easier. So, what is stopping us?

> We all have it within our power to modify the way we live in ways that are more sustainable.

Different Actions—Different Futures

What are you going to tell your children when they ask what you did to stop global warming? Will you tell them a little white lie? Or will you confess that you knew about the threat but did not make an effort to do anything about it? How do you think that will go over?

Fortunately for us, our children's future is not yet set in stone. Many doomsayers out there already think it is too late to avert catastrophe. The good news is that scientists believe there is still time for humanity to make smart choices that can mitigate the worst effects of climate change. It is still possible to choose for ourselves and our children the future direction of global warming. *The Climate Diet* provides all the knowledge and tools you need to significantly reduce your personal contribution and that of your family to climate change. Do it for yourself. Do it for your community. Do it for the future.

Appendices

Appendix A

More on the Science of Climate Change

Since 1990 the IPCC, sponsored by the United Nations, has been intensively studying the problem of climate change. Over the years this scientific body has developed a number of computer-based "emissions scenarios" to predict how certain types of policy and lifestyle actions will affect regional global surface, water, and atmospheric temperatures and other associated events. While the complexity of these models has advanced considerably over the years, their main findings have remained similar; namely, that higher GHG concentrations lead to warming, and human-caused GHG emissions are the main contributor to this problem. Also, as more information has become available, each successive report has made upward revisions in future temperature predictions. How do we know these models are reliable predictors of future climate conditions? Scientists have 400,000 years of data to test their reliability. Numerous studies show that model predictions closely track actual data records at the global level (IPCC, 2001, 2007).

Let's look a bit more at what scientists are saying about the future that lies ahead of us. Table A.1 shows projected temperature variations associated with different types of future development scenarios. The baseline prediction model assumes there will be no increase in GHG emissions after 2000. Of course this is impossible. Despite all the talk about the Kyoto Protocol, global emissions actually increased by more than 20% between the 1990s and the 2000–2005 period. Also, notice that temperatures will continue to rise by as much as 1.6° F (0.9° C) even if 2000 emissions are held constant. This is because GHG emissions often have a delayed effect on global temperatures. Therefore, much of our current warming is caused by pre-1970s emissions.

This "no increase" scenario is followed by what is called the A1 family of models. These models posit a world of fast economic expansion, population growth that peaks midcentury and then begins to decline, and the rapid introduction of new technologies. They also assume increased economic, social, and cultural convergence among regions. A1T (alternative technologies) assumes that most energy will eventually come from nonfossil energy sources. A1B (balanced energy sources) posits that energy consumption will be balanced between fossil and alternative sources. Finally, A1FI (fossil fuel–intensive) hypothesizes that fossil fuels will remain our primary energy source throughout the period (this is the model that most applies to our current world).

Table A.1 Projected Temperature Change for Various IPCC Scenarios: 1990s–2090s

Model Name	Best Model Temperature Estimate (AD 2090–2099)	Possible Temperature Range (AD 2090–2099)
No increase in GHG concentrations (baseline)	0.6° C (1.1° F)	0.3–0.9° C (0.5–1.6° F)
A1T (alternative technologies) scenario	2.4° C (4.3° F)	1.4–3.8° C (2.5–6.9° F)
A1B (balanced energy sources) scenario	2.8° C (5.0° F)	1.7–4.4° C (3.1–7.9° F)
A1FI (fossil fuel–intensive) scenario	4.0° C (7.2° F)	2.4–6.4° C (4.3–11.5° F)

Source: IPCC, 2007.

Table A.2 Temperature Variations 1990s and 2090s in Selected North American Cities

City	Average Mid-July High (July 15–20).	Mid-July (Lowest Recorded)	Mid-July (Highest Recorded)	Average Mid-July High, A1FI Scenario* (2090–2099)
Miami	32.2° C (90° F)	26.7° C (80° F)	36.7° C (98° F)	36.2° C (97° F)
Chicago	30.5° C (87° F)	20.5° C (69° F)	35.5° C (96° F)	34.5° C (94° F)
Houston	33.9° C (93° F)	27.2° C (81° F)	38.3° C (101° F)	37.9° C (100° F)
Las Vegas	40.0° C (104° F)	27.2° C (81° F)	47.2° C (117° F)	44.0° C (111° F)
Toronto	25.0° C (77° F)	18.9° C (66° F)	32.8° C (91° F)	29.0° C (84° F)
New York City	29.9° C (84° F)	20.5° C (69° F)	35.0° C (95° F)	33.9° C (93° F)
Washington DC	32.2° C (90° F)	24.4° C (76° F)	40.0° C (104° F)	36.2° C (97° F)
Atlanta	32.8° C (91° F)	27.8° C (82° F)	36.7° C (98° F)	36.8° C (98° F)

Note: *Assumes 4.0° C (7.2° F) average increase in temperature.

Source: Weather Underground, 2007.

Notice what happens if we continue along our trajectory of high-growth and high fossil fuel use. Global temperatures could increase between 4.3° F (2.4° C) and 11.5° F (6.4° C) in 100 years. In chapter 2 we learned that a temperature increase of less than 1.6° F (1.0° C) is already wreaking havoc on the Northwest's climate. It is endangering the snowpack and causing drought conditions all over the region. Can you imagine what an 11.5° F (6.4° C) change would do? Furthermore, all the IPCC models predict that temperatures in North America will increase more than the global mean with higher latitudes experiencing the most significant upsurge (IPCC, 2007).

If you think that Las Vegas is already hot during the summer you have not seen anything yet! Table A.2 provides a summary of observed and predicted temperature ranges for eight North American cities. I know many of you live in or near one of these cities. You know what normal summer heat feels like. You know how it affects your daily life; your house, your car, your yard, and your community. What will happen to the water supply, crops in the field, or farm animals if summer temperatures increase by 11.5° F (6.4° C)?

What happens when you add humidity to the mix? If you add the additional heat to the highest recorded temperature, things get even scarier. Can you imagine 126° F (52.2° C) in Las Vegas or 108° F (42.2° C) in Houston (with 80% humidity)?

Is this the future you want for your children? What would happen if you did not have access to electricity as is currently the case in many parts of the developing world? How would you survive the summer heat without air-conditioning? How will the billions of people who currently do not have electricity survive? The average core temperature of a human is 98.6° F (37.0° C). Only the healthiest person can maintain a core temperature of more than 104° F (40.0° C) for any length of time without complications (not factoring in humidity). And I have barely mentioned any of the other future effects of climate change discussed in chapters 1 and 2; that is, flooding, extreme weather, desertification, and so on.

The IPCC presents one additional set of scenarios that provide another path into the future. Scenario B1 predicts that higher levels of international cooperation coupled with less resource-intensive and sustainable social, political, and economic development could reduce by half the upward march of global temperatures. B1 provides a best estimate prediction of a 3.2° F (1.8° C) increase by 2100 with the overall possible range between 2.0 and 5.2° F (1.1 and 2.9° C). In other words, leading more environmentally responsible lifestyles will not only save the planet, but will foster the development of a more equitable and sustainable world. Sounds like a good deal to me.

Appendix B

Sample Climate Diet Worksheet

Table B.1 Current—'where you are'

Item/service	Watts	Usage hours/day	Usage days/yr	kWh/yr	GHG factor	CO_2/yr (lbs)	CO_2/yr (kg)
Computer	42.4	4	351	59.5	1.36	81.1	36.8
Stereo (desk)	15	3	351	15.8	1.36	21.5	9.8
Lamp with 60W bulb (1)	60	4	351	84.2	1.36	114.8	52.1
Lamp with 150W bulb (1)	150	4	351	210.6	1.36	287.0	130.2
Other Item 1				0.0	1.36	0.0	0.0
Other item 2				0.0	1.36	0.0	0.0
Other item 3				0.0	1.36	0.0	0.0
Other item 4				0.0	1.36	0.0	0.0
Total						504.5	228.9
Costs							
Total kWh used				370.2			
Cost per kWh in $ or your currency				0.1065			
Total cost to you in your currency				39.42			
GHG factors and electricity cost for selected regions					(lbs)	$ Cost/kWh	
Australia					1.72	0.0985	
Canada					0.48	0.0676	
Germany					1.12	0.2124	
S. Korea					0.99	0.1034	
United States					1.363	0.1065	
UK					1.02	0.2205	

Table B.2 Future—'where you want to be'

Item/service	Watts	Usage hours/ day	Usage days/yr	kWh/yr	GHG factor	CO_2/yr (lbs)	CO_2/yr (kg)	CO_2 saving (lbs)	CO_2 savings (kg)	CO_2 cut
Computer	42.4	4	351	59.5	1.36	81.1	36.8	0.0	0.0	0%
Stereo (desk)	15	3	351	15.8	1.36	21.5	9.8	0.0	0.0	0%
Lamp with 60 W bulb	15	4	351	21.1	1.36	28.7	13.0	86.1	39.1	75%
Lamp with 150 W bulb	38	4	351	53.4	1.36	72.7	33.0	214.3	97.2	75%
Other Item 1				0.0	1.36	0.0	0.0	0.0	0.0	0
Other item 2				0.0	1.36	0.0	0.0	0.0	0.0	0
Other item 3				0.0	1.36	0.0	0.0	0.0	0.0	0
Other item 4				0.0	1.36	0.0	0.0	0.0	0.0	0
Total						204.1	92.6			60%
Costs								Cost savings		23.48
Total kWh used				149.7						
Cost per kWh in $ or your currency				0.107						
Total cost to you				15.95						

Directions for filling out the worksheets on www.climatediet.com/tables.asp.

Fill in all of the red boxes, all other values will be calculated automatically.

Step 1: Enter the room/zone name. This will be automatically carried over to summary tables 9.1 and 9.2.

Step 2: 'Item/service' cell: List all items in your room/zone i.e. 'stereo'. In this case, items /services that will be changed to reduce energy use are underlined (changing to CFL bulbs).

Step 3: 'Watts' cell: See appendix E for typical wattage used by various products, check your product manual or check the product itself to see wattage listing (it is usually listed on the back or bottom of the product).

Step 4: 'Usage hours/day' cell: List the average number of hours per day you use this product. You can use the suggested usage values listed in appendix E or put in your own (be honest!).

Step 5: 'kWh/yr' cell: This is automatically calculated so do nothing.

Step 6: GHG Factor: Australia 1.90; Canada 0.486; Germany 1.12; S. Korea 0.99; United States 1.363; UK 1.02

Step 7: 'CO_2/yr (lbs)' and 'CO_2/yr (kg)' cells: These are automatically calculated so do nothing.

Step 8: $ Electricity kWh: Australia 0.0985; Canada 0.0676; Germany 0.2124; S. Korea 0.1034; United States 0.1065; UK 0.2205.

Step 9: Repeat steps 1–8 for each room/zone. Total CO_2 and cost savings by room and the grand total for your entire house/apartment are automatically calculated on tables 9.1 'How did you do? CO_2 emissions' and 9.2 'How did you do? Cost'. Did you win a 'Gold medal?'

Appendix C

International Energy and Price Data for Selected Countries (2007)

Country	CO₂/PC	PC/kWh Year	$ Premium (L)	$ Diesel (L)	$ Natural Gas 10⁷ kcal GVC	$ Natural Gas 100,000 Btu	$ L Fuel Oil (1,000L)	$ Electricity (1) 1 kWh	CO₂/kWh Per kg	CO₂/kWh (GHG Factor) (lb)
UK			1.706	1.521	801.12	1.31	680.18	0.2205	0.464	1.0208
South Korea	9.61	7,391	1.515		659.24	1.54	921.75	0.1034	0.451	0.9922
Germany	10.29	7,030	1.645	1.193			668.51	0.2124	0.508	1.1176
Italy	9.15	6,808	1.529	1.197	829.24		1,382.38	0.2529	0.506	1.1132
France	6.22	7,689	1.562	1.123	751.77	1.65	764.42	0.1515	0.075	0.165
Japan			1.146	0.748	1,245.56		597.93	0.1833		
Spain	7.72	5,924	1.248	1.005	850.61	1.83	725.63	0.1647	0.396	0.8712
Canada	17.24	17,179	0.802	0.812	504.68	0.99	693.97	0.0676	0.221	0.4862
U.S.*	19.73	13,338	0.624	0.674	611.15	1.23	644.76	0.1065	0.62	1.363
Mexico	3.59	1,804	0.614	0.456	659.4	1.66		0.101	0.58	1.276
Australia	17.53	11,126	0.912					0.0985	0.868	1.9096
New Zealand	8.04	8,887	0.99	0.586	1,103.69	1.85		0.1471	0.166	0.3652

Note: CO₂/PC (per capita) in metric tons. Includes direct and indirect emissions sources.

(1) Electricity Rates for Households. Fuel oil refers to oil commonly used in household boilers/furnaces.

Prices are as of 2007. U.S. prices for electricity from 2007. U.S. CO_2/kWh data is from EPA, 2007a. 1 gal = 3.785 L. GCV = gross caloric value. 100,000 Btu = 1 therm.

Source: International Energy Agency (2006, 2007), *Key World Energy Statistics: 2006, 2007*, IEA, Paris; IEA (2005) *CO₂ Emissions From Fuel Consumption: 1971–2003*, IEA, Paris.

Appendix D

Energy Data and Emissions by State/Province (USA, Canada, and Australia)

U.S. State	Primary Fuel	$ Retail 2007 U.S. Cents	Emissions Factors lb/kWh
Alabama	Coal	9.25	1.30
Alaska	Gas	15.01	1.11
Arizona	Coal	9.72	1.28
Arkansas	Coal	8.73	1.22
California	Gas	14.59	0.70
Colorado	Coal	9.19	1.99
Connecticut	Nuclear	18.81	0.75
Delaware	Coal	13.10	1.80
DC	Petrol	11.11	3.61
Florida	Gas	11.19	1.35
Georgia	Coal	9.20	1.39
Hawaii	Petrol	23.17	1.66
Idaho	Hydro	6.29	0.14
Illinois	Nuclear	10.33	1.16
Indiana	Coal	8.06	2.10
Iowa	Coal	9.41	1.94
Kansas	Coal	8.41	1.87
Kentucky	Coal	7.11	2.05
Louisiana	Gas	9.40	1.20
Maine	Gas	15.10	0.77
Maryland	Coal	11.47	1.29
Massachusetts	Gas	16.54	1.23
Michigan	Coal	10.34	1.41
Minnesota	Coal	9.02	1.59
Mississippi	Coal	9.39	1.41
Missouri	Coal	7.72	1.84
Montana	Coal	8.75	1.57
Nebraska	Coal	7.67	1.40
Nevada	Gas	11.69	1.57

U.S. State	Primary Fuel	$ Retail 2007 U.S. Cents	Emissions Factors lb/kWh
New Hampshire	Nuclear	14.86	0.78
New Jersey	Nuclear	14.59	0.71
New Mexico	Coal	8.99	1.99
New York	Nuclear	17.05	0.91
North Carolina	Coal	9.30	1.22
North Dakota	Coal	7.27	2.39
Ohio	Coal	9.59	1.78
Oklahoma	Coal	8.58	1.73
Oregon	Hydro	8.00	0.46
Pennsylvania	Coal	10.96	1.22
Rhode Island	Gas	13.88	1.07
South Carolina	Nuclear	9.17	0.92
South Dakota	Hydro	7.99	1.22
Tennessee	Coal	7.68	1.27
Texas	Gas	12.48	1.47
Utah	Coal	8.28	2.12
Vermont	Nuclear	14.09	0.07
Virginia	Coal	8.77	1.21
Washington	Hydro	7.14	0.36
West Virginia	Coal	6.55	1.99
Wisconsin	Coal	10.72	1.71
Wyoming	Coal	7.73	2.28
U.S. Average	Coal	10.65	1.36

Canada	Emission Factors	
	kg/kWh	lb/kWh
	(2002)	
Alberta	0.985	2.17
British Columbia	0.032	0.07
Manitoba	0.018	0.04
New Brunswick	0.571	1.26
Newfoundland/Labrador	0.286	0.63
Nunavut	0.2	0.44
Nova Scotia	0.961	2.11
Ontario	0.304	0.67
Prince Edward Island	0.72	1.58
Quebec	0.0093	0.02
Saskatchewan	0.888	1.95
Yukon	0.765	1.68
Canadian Average	**0.221**	**0.486**
Australia	Emission Factors	
	kg/kWh (2005)	lb/kWh
NSW or ACT	0.893	1.96
VIC	1.239	2.73
QLD	0.903	1.99
SA	0.865	1.90
WA	0.84	1.85
TAS	0.05	0.11
NT	0.682	1.50
Australian average	**0.86**	**1.91**

Source: Energy Information Administration (2007) *State Electricity Profiles*, Energy Information Administration, Washington DC; EIA (2006) *Electric Power Annual*, Energy Information Administration, Washington DC; EPA (2007a) EIA (December 2007) "Average retail prices to customers by end use sector by state: year to date," *Electric Power Monthly*, available at www.eia.doe.gov/cneaf/electricity/epm/table5_6_b.html.

Canadian and Australian values are for CO_2e emissions. Canadian values are from Stoyke (2007). Australian values from Australian Greenhouse Office (2006) *AGO Factors and Methods Workbook*, AGO, Sydney.

Appendix E(a)

Detailed Energy-Use Characteristics by Product/Item

Item	Low W	Medium W	High W	Hours/ day	Days/ year	kWh/ year (medium)	CO₂/ year (medium)	Cost/ year (medium)
Living/Bedroom								
Aquarium	50	65	1,200	24	365	569.4	776.1	60.6
Ceiling fan (w/out light)	60	75	175	3	351	79.0	107.6	8.4
Clock		2		24	365	17.5	23.9	1.9
DVD/VCR	2.93	7.1	10	0.8	351	2.0	2.7	0.2
Electric blanket (low given)	60	80	100	4	120	28.8	39.3	3.1
Portable heater	750	1,000	1,500	4	120	480.0	654.2	51.1
Satellite/cable box		20		4	351	28.1	38.3	3.0
Satellite dish		15		5	351	26.3	35.9	2.8
Stereo (large)	70	200	400	3	351	210.6	287.0	22.4
Stereo (desktop)		15		3	351	15.8	21.5	1.7
Stereo (boom box)		7		1	351	2.5	3.3	0.3
TV 19 in		110		4	351	154.4	210.5	16.4
TV 27 in		113		4	351	158.7	216.2	16.9
TV 36 in		133		4	351	186.7	254.5	19.9
TV 53 in		170		4	351	238.7	325.3	25.4
TV flat screen 37 in		120		4	351	168.5	229.6	17.9
Waterbed heater	750	1,000	1,500	4	120	480.0	654.2	51.1
Window fan	55	100	250	2	120	24.0	32.7	2.6
Video game console		20		2	351	14.0	19.1	1.5

Appendix E(b)

Detailed Energy-Use Characteristics by Product/Item

Item	Low W	Medium W	High W	Hours/ day	Days/ year	kWh/ year (medium)	CO$_2$/ year (medium)	Cost/ year (medium)
Heating and Cooling								
Air-conditioning (room)	1,900	3,000	5,000	8	120	2,880.0	3,925.4	306.4
Humidifier (room)	24	75	300	2	351	52.7	71.8	5.6
Dehumidifier (room)		350	785	2	351	245.7	334.9	26.1
Fan heater		2000		3	180	1,080.0	1,472.0	114.9
Portable fan (room)		30		3	351	31.6	43.1	3.4
Electronic air cleaner		50		2	351	35.1	47.8	3.7
Radiator (oil filled)		2,000		3	180	1,080.0	1,472.0	1,14.9
Bathroom								
Curling iron		90		0.17	351	5.4	7.3	0.6
Electric toothbrush		1.5		0.02	351	0.0	0.0	0.0
Hair dryer	700	1,200	1,875	0.25	351	105.3	143.5	11.2
Shaver		3		0.03	351	0.0	0.0	0.0
Vent fan		60		2	351	42.1	57.4	4.5
Lighting (Incandescent/CFL)								
40 W or 10 W	10	40		4	351	56.2	76.5	6.0
60 W or 15 W	15	60		4	351	84.2	114.8	9.0
75 W or 20 W	20	75		4	351	105.3	143.5	11.2
100 W or 29 W	29	100		4	351	140.4	191.4	14.9
150 W or 38 W	38	150		4	351	210.6	287.0	22.4

Appendix E(c)

Detailed Energy Use Characteristics by Product/Item

Item	Low W	Medium W	High W	Hours/ day	Days/ year	kWh/ year (medium)	CO_2/ year (medium)	Cost/ year (medium)
Kitchen/Small Appliances								
Air corn popper		1,400		0.08	52	5.8	7.9	0.6
Blender		300		0.02	351	2.1	2.9	0.2
Bread maker		680		2	52	70.7	96.4	7.5
Coffeemaker	900	1,200	1,500	0.25	351	105.3	143.5	11.2
Broiler		1,500		0.25	351	131.6	179.4	14.0
Can opener		100		0.02	351	0.7	1.0	0.1
Deep fryer		1,000		0.4	351	140.4	191.4	14.9
Electronic frying pan		1,200		0.5	351	210.6	287.0	22.4
Electronic knife		95		0.17	351	5.7	7.7	0.6
Espresso machine		360		0.17	351	21.5	29.3	2.3
Food processor		800		0.17	351	47.7	65.1	5.1
Garbage disposal		750		0.03	351	7.9	10.8	0.8
Instant hot water dispenser		18		24	351	151.6	206.7	16.1
Juicer		450		0.2	251	22.6	30.8	2.4
Kettle (electric)	750	1,500	2,200	0.25	351	131.6	179.4	14.0
Kettle (Japanese 2 L)		900		0.25	351	79.0	107.6	8.4
Microwave	750	1,000	1,500	0.25	351	87.8	119.6	9.3
Coffee percolator		600		0.42	351	88.5	120.6	9.4
Rice cooker (5 cups)		650		0.5	351	114.1	155.5	12.1
Slow cooker		200		6	52	62.4	85.1	6.6
Toaster	600	1,100	1,400	0.1	351	38.6	52.6	4.1
Toaster oven		1,200		0.25	351	105.3	143.5	11.2
Trash compactor		400		0.33	351	46.3	63.2	4.9
Water cooler (hot/cold)	50	91	150	24	365	797.2	1,086.5	84.8

Appendix E(d)

Detailed Energy Use Characteristics by Product/Item

Item	Low W	Medium W	High W	Hours/ day	Days/ year	kWh/ year (medium)	CO₂/ year (medium)	Cost/ year (medium)
Kitchen/Large Appliances								
Refrigerator 23 cu ft	65	76	100	24	365	665.8	907.4	70.8
Side mount with ice								
Freezer 22 cu ft	64	71	100	24	365	622.0	847.7	66.2
Dishwasher	700	1,200	2,400	0.6	351	252.7	344.5	26.9
Range stove top	1,200	2,500		1	351	877.5	1,196.0	93.4
Range oven		2,600	3,500	1	351	912.6	1,243.9	97.1
Wash/Dry/Utility								
Doorbell		5		24	365	43.8	59.7	4.7
Garage door opener		6		24	365	52.6	71.6	5.6
Gutter heater		900		2	180	324.0	441.6	34.5
Iron	900	1,200		0.12	351	50.5	68.9	5.4
Washer	375	450	600	0.8	351	126.4	172.2	13.4
Instant heater (electric)		900		2	351	631.8	861.1	67.2
Vacuum cleaner (central)	700	1,200	1,700	0.12	52	7.5	10.2	0.8
Vacuum cleaner (hand)		300		0.03	351	3.2	4.3	0.3
Vacuum cleaner (upright)		650		0.12	351	27.4	37.3	2.9
Water pump (deep 0.5 hp)		300		2	351	210.6	287.0	22.4
Water pump (deep 1 hp)		600		2	351	421.2	574.1	44.8
Water tank (50 gal)	500	550		24	365	4,818.0	6,566.9	512.6
Wash machine (kWh/L)	0.6	1.35	2.26	1	392	529.2	721.3	56.3
Dryer (kWh/L)	1.01	2.26	2.33	1	392	885.9	1,207.5	94.3

Appendix E(e)

Detailed Energy Use Characteristics by Product/Item

Item	Low W	Medium W	High W	Hours/ day	Days/ year	kWh/ year (medium)	CO_2/ year (medium)	Cost/ year (medium)
Home Office								
Computer (adjusted Energy Star)	40.2	42.4	70	4	264	44.8	61.0	4.8
Printer	16.6	42.7	100	2	264	22.5	30.7	2.4
Radio	15	30	50	2	351	21.1	28.7	2.2
Fan	25	30	60	3	351	31.6	43.1	3.4
Fax	23.4	36.6		4	264	38.6	52.7	4.1
Copier	75.2	85.3		4	264	90.1	122.8	9.6
LCD 19 in	11.3	52.6		4	264	55.5	75.7	5.9
Yard								
Chainsaw		1,800		0.17	30	9.2	12.5	1.0
Circular saw		1,200		0.17	52	10.6	14.5	1.1
Electric lawn mower		1,500		1	30	45.0	61.3	4.8
Leaf blower		2,500		0.17	26	11.1	15.1	1.2
Outdoor electric grill		1,800		0.25	120	54.0	73.6	5.7
Pool heater/electronic		50,000		6	90	27,000.0	36,801.0	2,872.8
Pool heater/heat pump		12,000		6	90	6,480.0	8,832.2	689.5
Pool pump 0.75 hp		750		6	90	405.0	552.0	43.1
Pool pump 2 hp		2,000		6	90	1,080.0	1,472.0	1,14.9
Power washer		2,000		0.17	90	30.6	41.7	3.3
Weed trimmer		500		1	30	15.0	20.4	1.6

Source: European Commission Joint Research Center (2005) *Energy, Lifestyles and Climate Technical Report*, Brussels, Belgium, European Commission.

Ireland Electricity Supply Board (2007) "Appliance Calculator," available at www.esb.ie/main/home/index.jsp.

Natural Resources Canada (2006) *EnerGuide Appliance Directory*, Natural Resources Canada, Ottawa.

Natural Resources Canada (2006) *Purchasing Tool Kit: A Guide to Buying Energy Star Qualified Products*, Natural Resources Canada, Ottawa.

Pacific Gas and Electric (2007) "Energy Costs for Selected Appliances," available at www.pge.com/.

U.S. Department of Energy (2007) "Energy Star Program Cost Worksheets," available at www.energystar.gov. Also visit www.eere.energy.gov/consumer/.

Appendix F

CO$_2$e Emissions Associated with Farming and Animal Husbandry

Item	Grams CO$_2$e per kg Product	Pounds CO$_2$e per kg Product
Meat		
Beef cattle (farm)	11,600	25.52
Beef (tenderloin-retail)	68,000	149.60
Beef (top round-retail)	42,300	93.06
Pig (farm)	2,250	4.95
Pork (tenderloin-retail)	4,560	10.03
Pork (ham shank-retail)	2,950	6.49
Chicken (farm)	1,860	4.09
Chicken (uncut-retail)	31,60	6.95
Fish		
Trout (living-farmed)	1,800	3.96
Trout (farmed-retail)	4,470	9.83
Cod (frozen-retail)	3,200	7.04
Lobster	20,200	44.44
Shrimp (frozen peeled-retail)	10,500	23.10
Shrimp (fresh-retail)	3,000	6.60
Dairy		
Milk (L)	1,200	2.64
Cheese (yellow-retail)	180	0.40
Breads and Cereals		
Bread (wheat bakery)	780	1.72
Bread (wheat packaged)	840	1.85
Bread (frozen-retail)	1,200	2.64
Soybeans	620	1.36
Oats	570	1.25
Spring barley	650	1.43
Wheat	710	1.56
Vegetables		
Tomatos (retail)	3,450	7.59
Onions (retail)	380	0.84
Carrots (retail)	120	0.26
Potatos (retail)	220	0.48
Sugar beets (retail)	160	0.35

Source: Life Cycle Analysis (2006), "LCA Food Database," Danish Environmental Protection Agency, Copenhagen, Denmark, available at www.lcafood.dk.

References

References

Chapter 1

Appenzeller, T., and Dimick, D. (2004). "The heat is on," *National Geographic*, vol. 206, pp.145–152.

Baumert, K., Herzog, T., and Pershing, J. (eds.). (2005). *Navigating the Numbers: Greenhouse Gas Data and International Climate Policy*, World Resources Institute, Washington DC.

Bush, G. (2006). 'Transcript of President Bush's State of the union address', CNN.com, 31 January, available at http://edition.cnn.com/2006/POLITICS/01/31/sotu.transcript/

International Energy Agency (IEA). (2007). *World Energy Outlook: 2007, Executive Summary, China and India Insights*, IEA, Paris, available at www.iea.org/Textbase/npsum/WEO2007SUM.pdf

Intergovernmental Panel on Climate Change. (IPCC). (2007). *Climate Change 2007: The Physical Science Basis—Summary for Policymakers*, IPCC, Paris, available at http://ipcc-wg1.ucar.edu/wg1/wg1-report.html

Intergovernmental Panel on Climate Change (IPCC). (2001). *IPCC Third Assessment Report: Climate Change 2001*, R. Watson et al. (eds.). Cambridge University Press, Cambridge, UK.

New York Times. (2007). "72 degree day breaks record in New York," *New York Times*, 7 January, available at www.nytimes.com/2007/01/07/nyregion/07heat.html?ex=1325826000&en=97644d1f9ec8c3c6&ei=5088

Rosenthal, E. and Revkin, A. (2007). "Science panel calls global warming unequivocal," *New York Times*, 3 February, available at www.nytimes.com/2007/02/03/science/earth/03climate.html?_r=1&scp=1&sq=global+warming+IPCC+weather+extremes&st=nyt&oref=slogin

Science Daily. (2007). "IPCC report—the arctic: thawing permafrost, melting sea ice and more significant changes," Science Daily, 11 April, available at www.sciencedaily.com/releases/2007/04/070410140922.htm

The Economist. (2007). "Australia's water shortage: the big dry," *The Economist*, 26 April, available at www.economist.com/world/displaystory.cfm?story_id=9071007

World Resources Institute (WRI). (2006). CAIT Climate Database, WRI, Washington DC, available at http://cait.wri.org/

Chapter 2

Ahmed, A., Alam M., et al. (1999). "Adaptation to climate change in Bangladesh: future outlook," in S. Huq, Z. Karim, M. Asaduzzaman, and F. Mahtab (eds.), *Vulnerability and Adaptation to Climate Change for Bangladesh*, Klewer Academic Publishers, Boston, pp.125–144.

Appenzeller, T. (2004). "The end of cheap oil?" *National Geographic*, available at http://magma.nationalgeographic.com/ngm/0406/feature5/

BBC. (2001). "Iceland launches energy revolution," BBC.com, 24 December, available at http://news.bbc.co.uk/2/hi/science/nature/1727312.stm

Brown, L. (2006). "The population-environment nexus," paper delivered at 2006 International Parliamentarians' Conference on the Implementation of the ICPD Programme of Action and sponsored by the United Nations Population Fund, Bangkok, Thailand, 21–22 November, available at www.unfpa.org/parliamentarians/documents/IPCIpaperBrown.doc

Brown, L. (2005). *Plan B*, Norton, New York.

Bruntland Commission. (1987). *Our Common Future*, Oxford University Press, Cambridge, UK.

Byrd, D., Block, J., Patterson, L., and Salzar, J. (2003), "Rising sea forces islanders to relocate," Earth and Sky Radio Series, 31 March, available at www.earthsky.org/radioshows/49296/rising-sea-forces-islanders-to-relocate

Carson, Rachel. (1967). *Silent Spring*, Fawcett Publications, New York.

Castles, S. (2002). "Environmental change and forced migration: making sense of the debate," *New Issues in Refugee Research*, Working Paper #70, Refugees Study Centre, Oxford, UK. Report distributed by the Evaluation and Policy Analysis Unit, United Nations High Commissioner for Refugees, available at www.unhcr.org/research/RESEARCH/3de344fd9.pdf

Evangelical Environmental Network. (1994). "On the care of creation: an evangelical declaration on the care of creation," Evangelical Environmental Network, available at www.creationcare.org/resources/declaration.php

Goodland, R., and Ledee, G. (1987). "Neo-classical economics and principles of sustainable development," *Ecological Modeling*, vol. 38, pp.19–47.

Gottlieb, R. (2006). *A Greener Faith: Religious Environmentalism and Our Planet's Future*, Oxford University Press, New York.

Hardin, G. (1968). "The tragedy of the commons," *Science*, vol. 162 (December), pp.1243–1260.

International Institute for Sustainable Development (IISD). (2002). "Summary of the sixteenth session of the subsidiary bodies to the un framework convention on climate change," *Earth Negotiations Bulletin*, 17 June, vol. 12, p. 200, available at www.iisd.ca/climate/sb16/index.html

Leopold, A. (1968). *A Sand County Almanac: And Sketches Here and There*, quoted in Andrew Dobson (ed.) (1991) *The Green Reader: Essays Toward a Sustainable Society*, p. 238. Mercury House, San Francisco.

Lovelock, J. (2006). *The Revenge of Gaia: Earth's Climate Crisis and the Fate of Humanity*, Basic Books, New York.

National Climatic Data Center/National Oceanic and Atmospheric Administration (NCDC/NOAA). (2006). *Climate of 2005 Wildfire Season Summary*, NCDC/NOAA, Washington DC.

National Oceanic and Atmospheric Administration (NOAA). (2006). "Selected U.S. city and state extremes, January 2006," available at www.ncdc.noaa.gov/oa/climate/research/2006/jan/januaryext2006.html

Northwest Weather and Avalanche Center (NWAC). (2006). *Historical NWAC Snow Depth Data and Plots*, NWAC, Seattle, available at www.nwac.us/mtnweather.htm

Parker, G., Bounds, A., and Benoit, B. (2007). "EU seizes leadership of climate fight," *Financial Times*, 10 March, p. 2.

Peterson, K. (1998). "Environmental ethics in interreligious perspective," in Twiss, S. et al. (ed.), *Explorations in Global Ethics: Comparative Religious Ethics and Interreligious Dialogue*, Westview Press, Boulder, CO.

Point Carbon. (2007). "Carbon 2007—a new climate for carbon trading," Røine, K., and H. Hasselknippe (eds.). *Point Carbon*, Oslo, Norway.

Puget Sound Action Team. (2005). *Uncertain Future: Climate Change and its Effects on the Puget Sound*, State of Washington, Seattle.

Saunders, S., and Maxwell, M. (2005). *Less Snow, Less Water: Climate Disruption in the West*, Rocky Mountain Climate Coalition, Washington DC.

Twitchell, J. (1999). *Lead Us into Temptation: The Triumph of American Materialism*, Columbia University Press, New York.

White, Lynn. (1967). "The historical roots of our ecological crisis," *Science*, vol. 155, pp.1203+.

World Resources Institute (WRI). (2006). Climate Analysis Indicators Tool, WRI, Washington DC, available at http://cait.wri.org/

Chapter 3

Energy Information Administration (EIA). (December 2007). "Table 5.6.B. Average retail price of electricity to ultimate customers by end-use sector, by state, year-to-date through September 2007 and 2006," *Electric Power Monthly*, available at www.eia.doe. gov/cneaf/electricity/epm/table5_6_b.html

Environmental Protection Agency (EPA). (2007a). "eGRID 2006: Year 2004 state emissions," EPA, Washington DC, available at www.epa.gov/ cleanenergy/energy-resources/egrid/index.html

Environmental Protection Agency (EPA). (2007b). *U.S. Greenhouse Gas Inventory Reports, Inventory of U.S. Greenhouse Gas Emissions and Sinks: 1990–2005*, EPA, Washington DC, available at www.epa.gov/ climatechange/emissions/usinventoryreport.html

Environmental Protection Agency (EPA). (2007c). *Fuel Economy Guide*: Model Year 2008, EPA, Washington DC, available at www.fueleconomy. gov

International Energy Agency (IEA). (2006). Key World Energy Statistics. IEA, Paris, France.

Chapter 4

Carbonneutral. (2006). *Comprehensive Calculator Background Information*, Carbonneutral, Sydney, Australia.

Consumer Research Council. (2005). *Save Money and Save the Environment: A Consumer's Guide to Energy Efficient Products for the Home*, Consumer Research Council, Washington DC.

Cubarrubia, E. (2006). "LCDs to dominate TV market," Red Herring, available at www.redherring.com/Article.aspx?a=20202&hed=LCDs +to+Dominate+TV+Market

Energy Star. (2006). "Office equipment," available at http://www.energystar. gov/index.cfm?fuseaction=find_a_product.showProductCategory& pcw_code=OEF

Environmental Protection Agency (EPA). (2007). "How do we use water," available at www.epa.gov/WaterSense/water/save/use.htm

Goodal, C. (2007). *How to Live a Low-Carbon Life: The Individual's Guide to Stopping Climate Change*, Earthscan, London

Natural Resources Canada (NRC). (2004). *Keeping the Heat In*, NRC, Ottawa.

Natural Resources Canada (NRC). (2006). *Purchasing Tool Kit: A Guide to Buying Energy Star Qualified Products*, NRC, Ottawa.

U.S. Department of Energy. (2007). 2007 Buildings Energy Data Book, U.S. Department of Energy, Washington DC.

Chapter 5

Energy Star. (2007a). "Air conditioners," available at www.energystar.gov/index.cfm?c=heat_cool.pr_hvac

Energy Star. (2007b). "Recommended levels of insulation," available at www.energystar.gov/index.cfm?c=home_sealing.hm_improvement_insulation_table

Goodall, C. (2007). *How to Live a Low-Carbon Life: The Individual's Guide to Stopping Climate Change*, Earthscan, London.

Johnson, D., and Master, K. (2004). *Green Remodeling: Changing the World One Room at a Time*, New Society Publishers, Gabriola Island, British Columbia, Canada.

National Wildlife Federation. (2006). "Create a certified wildlife habitat," National Wildlife Federation, Washington DC, available at www.nwf.org/backyard/70000goal.cfm

Pacific Gas and Electric. (2007). "Energy-saving resources," Pacific Gas and Electric, available at www.pge.com/res/rebates/energy_tools_resources/

Chapter 6

Appenzeller, T., and Dimick, D. (2004). "The heat is on," *National Geographic*, vol. 206, no. 3, pp. 2–11.

Environmental Protection Agency (EPA). (2007). "Composting," EPA, available at www.epa.gov/epaoswer/non-hw/composting/index.htm

Environmental Protection Agency (EPA). (2003). *Municipal Solid Waste Generation, Recycling and Disposal in the United States*, EPA, Washington DC.

Gershon, D. (2006). *Low Carbon Diet: A 30 Day Program to Lose 5000 Pounds*, Empowerment Institute, Woodstock, NY.

Goodall, J. (2005). *Harvest for Hope: A Guide to Mindful Eating*, Warner Wellness Books, New York.

Harrington, J. (2005). "Panda diplomacy, state environmentalism, international relations and Chinese foreign policy," in P. Harris (ed.), *Environmental Politics in East and Southeast Asia*, Earthscan/UNU Press, Tokyo and London.

Heavey, S. (2007). "Petfood recall widens cross-contamination," Reuters.com American.com, 6 May, available at www.reuters. com/article/healthNews/idUSN0326662720070506

Murray, S. (2007). "The end of the road for food miles?" *Financial Times*, 29 April, Life and Arts Section, p. 2.

Natural Trails and Water Coalition. (2007) "BLM and off-road vehicles," available at www.naturaltrails. org/about-us/issues-were-working-on/bureau-of-land-management/

Newdream. (2005). "Holiday and tips resources," Center for a New American Dream, available at www.newdream.org/holiday/tips.php

Reay, D. (2005). *Climate Change Begins at Home*, Macmillan, New York.

Royte, E. (2005). *Garbage Land: The Secret Trail of Trash*, Back Bay Books, New York.

Snohomish County Public Works. (2004). "Checklist for a lighter holiday," Snohomish County Public Works, Snohomish, WA.

The Carbon Trust. (2006). *Carbon Footprints in the Supply Chain: The Next Step for Business*, The Carbon Trust, London.

Tucson Citizen. (2007). "Off-road vehicles out of control, federal rangers say," 12 December 2007, available at www.tucsoncitizen.com/daily/ local/71256.php

Washington State Department of Ecology. (2004). *Master Composter/ Recycler Training Manual*, Department of Ecology, Olympia, WA.

Chapter 7

Bumiller E., and Nagourney, A. (2006). "Bush, resetting agenda, says U.S. must cut reliance on oil," *New York Times*, 1 February, available at www. nytimes.com/2006/02/01/politics/01bush.html?ei=5088&en=a4e9a812 2ffde6f7&ex=1296450000&partner=rssnyt&emc=rss&pagewanted=all

Daily Fuel Economy. (2007). "Daily fuel economy tip," Dailyfueleconomy. com, available at www.dailyfueleconomytip.com/index.php

Edmunds. (2007). "True cost to own estimates," available at www. edmunds.com/apps/cto/CTOintroController

Energy Information Administration (EIA). (2005). *The Annual Energy Outlook*, EIA, Washington DC.

Environmental Protection Agency/Department of Energy. (2007a). Find and Compare Cars Database, available at www.fueleconomy.gov/feg/ findacar.htm

Environmental Protection Agency/Department of Energy. (2007b). *Fuel Economy Guide: Model Year 2008*, EPA, Washington DC, available at www.fueleconomy.gov/feg/FEG2000.htm

European Climate Exchange. (2007). "ECX CFI futures contracts: Historic data, 2005–2008," European Climate Exchange, 2 April, available at www.europeanclimateexchange.com/index_noflash.php

European Commission, DG Environment. (2006). *Review and Analysis of the Reduction Potential and Costs of Technological and other Measures to Reduce CO_2-emissions from Passenger Cars*, European Commission, DG Environment, Brussels, Belgium.

European Commission, DG Environment (2005a) *Giving Wings to Emission Trading: Inclusion of Aviation Under the European Emission Trading System (ETS): Design and Impacts*, European Commission DG Environment, Delft, Netherlands.

European Commission, DG Environment. (2005b). *Reducing the Climate Change Impact of Aviation: Report on the Public Consultation on Reducing the Climate Change Impact of Aviation*, European Commission, DG Environment, Delft, Netherlands.

European Commission Joint Research Centre. (2005) *Energy, Lifestyles and Climate Technical Report*, European Commission, Brussels, Belgium.

European Environment Agency. (2005). "Are we moving in the right direction? Indicators on transport and environmental integration in the EU: Term 2000," *Environmental Issue Report #12*. European Environment Agency, available at http://reports.eea.europa.eu/ENVISSUENo12/en/page027.html

Gelbspan, R. (2004). *Boiling Point: How Politicians, Big Oil and Coal, Journalists, and Activists Are Fuelling the Climate Crisis—And What We Can Do to Avert Disaster*, Basic Books, New York.

Martin, E. (2007). "US stocks advance on takeovers; oil rises to $66, corn falls," Bloomberg.com, 2 April, available at www.bloomberg.com/apps/news?pid=20601087&sid=aRQci2DN_n.M&refer=home

Motavalli, J. (2007). "A universe of promise (and a tankful of caveats)," *New York Times*, 29 April, available at www.nytimes.com/2007/04/29/automobiles/29PRIMER.html

O'Keefe, E. (2006). "On the road again, where biodiesel is a rising star," *New York Times*, 5 July, available at www.nytimes.com/2006/07/05/business/05biowillie.html?_r=1&scp=2&sq=peanut%20oil%20biodiesel&st=nyt&oref=slogin

Point Carbon. (2007). "Carbon 2007—a new climate for carbon trading", K. Røine, and H. Hasselknippe (eds.). *Point Carbon*, Oslo, Norway

PR Newswire. (2007). "Corn based ethanol will have a vital role, but the cellulosic variety is unclear," PR Newswire, 3 September, available at www.chron.com/disp/story.mpl/business/5104798.html

Stoyke, G. (2007). *The Carbon Buster's Home Energy Handbook*, New Society Publishers, Gabriola Island, British Columbia, Canada.

World Changing. (2007). "The week in sustainable mobility," Worldchanging.com, 11 March, available at www.worldchanging.com/archives/006285.html

Chapter 8

Bayon, R. (2002). "More than hot air: Market solutions to global warming," *World Policy Journal*, vol 19, no. 3, p. 60–68.

Brown, L. (1995). *Who Will Feed China? Wake Up Call for a Small Planet*, W.W. Norton, New York.

Carbon Disclosure Project. (2007). *Carbon Disclosure Project 2007 Report: Global FT 500*, Carbon Disclosure Project, London.

Ceres. (2006) *Climate and Climate Change: Making the Direction*, Ceres, Washington DC.

Gore, A. West, B., and Guggenheim, D. (2006). *An Inconvenient Truth* (DVD), Paramount Pictures Hollywood, CA.

Heck, P., Bresch, D., and Trober, S. (2006). The effects of climate change: Storm damage in Europe on the rise," Swiss Re Zurich, available at www.swissre.com/resources/0e9e8a80455c7a86b1e4bb80a45d76a0-Publ06_Klimaveraenderung_en.pdf

High Wind. (2007). For more information about High Wind, contact Belden or Lisa Paulson at lpaulson@danet.com

Morningstar. (2006). "Socially responsible funds," Morningstar.com, available at http://screen.morningstar.com/FundSelector.html?fsection=ToolScreener

Northwest Environment Watch. (2004). Cascadia Scorecard: 2004, Northwest Environment Watch (now called Sightline Institute), Seattle, WA

Odell, A. (2007). "Grading sustainability reports: Creating the curve," SRI World Group, 4 May, available at www.socialfunds.com/news/article.cgi/2285.html

Pew Trust. (2006). *Getting Ahead of the Curve: Corporate Strategies that Address Climate Change*, Pew Trust, Washington DC.

Pfiefer, S. (2007). "Boeing's green sky thinking," *The Sunday Telegraph*, 22 April available at www.telegraph.co.uk/money/main.jhtml?xml=/money/2007/04/22/ccboeing22.xml

Sierra Club. (2005). "Partnerships promote corporate accountability," Sierra Club, available at www.sierraclub.org/partnerships/accountability/

Sightline Institute (2006). *Cascadia Scorecard: 2006*, Sightline Institute, Seattle, WA.

The Economist. (2007). "Shortages of turbines and polysilicon are holding back the clean-tech boom," 29 March, *The Economist*, available at www.economist.com/research/articlesBySubject/displaystory.cfm?subjectid=8780295&story_id=8935021

Vig, N. and Kraft M. (eds.). (2003) *Environmental Policy in the 21st Century*, Sage Press, Washington DC.

World Resources Institute (WRI). (2006). CAIT Climate Database, WRI, Washington DC, available at http://cait.wri.org/

Chapter 9

Kemp, W. (2004). *Smart Power: An Urban Guide to Renewable Energy and Efficiency*, Aztext Press, Tamworth, Ontario, Canada.

Chapter 10

Olesen, A. (2006). "Stephen Hawking warns about global warming," Associated Press, 22 June, available at www.enn.com/sci-tech/article/4525

Appendices

Intergovernmental Panel on Climate Change (IPCC). (2001). *IPCC Third Assessment Report: Climate Change 2001*, Cambridge University Press, Cambridge, UK.

Intergovernmental Panel on Climate Change (IPCC). (2007). *Climate Change 2007: The Physical Science Basis—Summary for Policymakers*, IPCC, Paris, France, available at http://ipcc-wg1.ucar.edu/index.html

Stoyke, G. (2007) The Carbon Busters Home Energy Handbook, Gabriola Island, New Society Publishers

The Weather Underground. (2007). Weather Underground Historical Weather Database, available at www.wunderground.com

About the Author

Jonathan Harrington is an associate professor of international relations at Troy University. An award-winning teacher, Jonathan has been educating students and the public about climate change and environmental issues for more than 15 years. He has published numerous articles and chapters on environment- and development-related topics. He has hosted, organized, and spoken at international conferences in Japan, New Zealand, China and Hong Kong, and the United States. His love for nature and overriding concern about the future of all the backyards he has had over the years—in Shanghai, London, Hyderabad, Taipei, Tokyo, and Utah, among others—is vividly expressed in his book. Jonathan lives with his wife and daughter in the Seattle area.

Index